Good Housekeeping

Brownies

Favorite Recipes for Blondies, Bars & Brownies

Almond Cheesecake Swirl Brownies (page 133)

Good Housekeeping

Brownies

Favorite Recipes for Blondies, Bars & Brownies

HEARST BOOKS

A division of Sterling Publishing Co., Inc.

New York / London

www.sterlingpublishing.com

This custom edition published by
World Publications Group, Inc.
140 Laurel Street
East Bridgewater, MA 02333
www.wrldpub.com

Originally published by Hearst Books in a different
format as *Good Housekeeping Brownies!*

Book design by Memo Productions

Photography credits on page 158

10 9 8 7 6 5 4 3 2 1

Hearst Books
A division of Sterling Publishing Co., Inc.
387 Park Avenue South
New York, NY 10016

Good Housekeeping is a registered trademark
of Hearst Communications, Inc.

www.goodhousekeeping.com

Manufactured in China

ISBN 978-1-57215-617-3

CONTENTS

Malted Milk Bars (page 28)

FOREWORD

Who can resist a brownie? These easy, one-batch bars are as American a tradition as apple pie and can be made in a fraction of the time. Whether you need a double batch for a bake sale or rich trufflelike confections for a fancy party, we've got a recipe for you. If you're in a real time crunch, we've converted some of our favorite from-scratch recipes to easy versions made from a brownie mix plus a few stir-ins. All of the recipes have been triple-tested in the *Good Housekeeping* Test Kitchens by our staff, so they're guaranteed to be good.

In *Brownies!* you will find goodies for all tastes. Yes, we know there are actually people who do not like chocolate. Our book of bars has lots of other luscious options, Fresh Lemon Bars, Cherry Cheesecake Triangles, and Caramel Pecan Bars among them. You can satisfy any craving with just a few supermarket ingredients, many of which are already in your pantry.

In addition to fabulous recipes, *Brownies!* will help you to become a better baker through general baking advice as well as tips specific to making, decorating, and storing your bar cookies. I love to individually wrap a few bars and freeze them for impromptu teatime treats.

Whatever the occasion, you'll find crowd-pleasers—chocolate, and not—in this collection of *Good Housekeeping*'s most popular brownies and bars, including irresistible new favorites. I hope *Brownies!* satisfies your sweet tooth and will become a well-used addition to your cookbook library.

SUSAN WESTMORELAND
Food Director, *Good Housekeeping*

INTRODUCTION

There are many reasons why brownies, blondies, and other bar cookies are so popular, the main one being that they are scrumptious. They are also so easy to whip up that even a beginning baker can get great results, and, unlike many other desserts, they require a minimum of ingredients, all readily available. Best of all, they take a relatively short time to prepare.

From simple to sophisticated, there is a bar cookie to suit every taste. Whether you are preparing something to bring to a school bake sale, to pack into the kids' lunch boxes, to ship overseas to a loved one, or to serve as a finale to dinner, you'll find a recipe here to fill the bill.

To make the process even easier and quicker, we've adapted some of our favorite recipes to take advantage of the excellent mixes now available in supermarkets. These recipes will be indicated by a shaded box just like this one (see, for example, Easy German Chocolate Brownies, page 43). We tested these recipes using a variety of store and brand names. Any plain brownie mix between 19½ and 22½ ounces, for a 13" by 9" baking pan, will work. Just be sure that the mix is either fudgy or chewy style and does not have any add-ins, such as nuts or caramel.

Getting Started

Before you begin, you should become familiar with some basic procedures that will help you get perfect results.

• Read the recipe all the way through before you start. Butter may have to be softened, nuts may need to be toasted, chocolate may need to be melted.

• Make sure that ingredients are at room temperature (68° to 70°F) unless otherwise indicated.

• Don't use a substitute for any ingredient unless one is specifically offered in the recipe.

• Measure everything! In baking, adding a pinch of this and a dash of that can lead to disaster. Recipes for baked goods are exact formulas, and what you add—or subtract—can adversely affect the taste and texture of the final product.

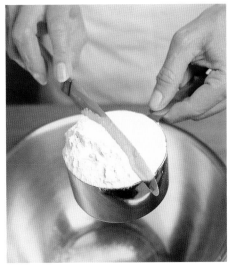

• Use dry measuring cups to measure dry ingredients and liquid measuring cups to measure liquid ingredients; the two kinds of cups don't hold the same volume. How you measure flour is particularly important: Stir the flour in the canister, then spoon it into a dry-cup measure and level it off with a straightedge, such as a metal spatula. Don't tap or pack it down, or your baked goods may turn out dry or, worse, rock hard.

Pantry

Brownies and other bar cookies require just a few ingredients, most of which you probably already have in your pantry or can find easily in your local supermarket.

Flour: Most recipes here call for all-purpose flour. One calls for cake flour (not self-rising, see Scottish Shortbread, page 69) and one calls for whole-wheat flour (see Whole-Wheat Fig Bars, page 81).

Sweeteners: granulated sugar, brown sugar, confectioners' sugar, honey, and corn syrup.

Dairy: butter or margarine (see page 10), eggs, milk, cream cheese, sour cream, and heavy or whipping cream.

Chocolate and cocoa: unsweetened, bittersweet, and semisweet, chocolate squares or bars; chocolate morsels; and unsweetened cocoa.

Flavorings: extracts, liqueurs, instant espresso-coffee powder.

Add-ins: nuts (see page 31 for how to toast nuts), mini marshmallows, coconut, dried fruits, and candies.

Fillings: jams, peanut butter, almond paste, and lemon curd.

A WORD ABOUT BUTTER

When a recipe calls for butter or margarine, we prefer salted butter. Don't substitute a reduced-fat spread or stick if a recipe calls for butter or margarine. Butter and margarine have 80 percent fat content; "lighter" products contain less, some as little as 25 percent, and using them would change the chemistry of the recipe. Use the "light" products only in those recipes that specifically call for them.

CHOOSING CHOCOLATE

Most supermarkets stock several brands of chocolate for baking. You don't have to blow your budget by purchasing a super-premium brand, but don't skimp on quality either. Always use the type and the amount of chocolate specified in the recipe.

• Unsweetened chocolate is virtually pure chocolate liquor in solid form, with no sugar added. It is sold in packages of 1-ounce squares.

• Semisweet chocolate contains some sugar (between 40 and 65 percent). It is sold in packages of 1-ounce squares or bars; the bars are generally better quality. Semisweet chocolate, chopped into chunks, can be substituted for semisweet chocolate chips.

• Since white chocolate does not contain chocolate liquor (and often substitutes palm kernel oil for cocoa butter), it is technically speaking, not chocolate. But it's delicious, so why fuss over technicalities? For the best white chocolate, look for cocoa butter in the ingredients.

• There are two types of unsweetened cocoa powder: alkalized (Dutch-processed) and nonalkalized. Dutch-processed cocoa has been treated with an alkali to neutralize its acidity, a process that creates a darker, less intensely flavored cocoa. Nonalkalized cocoa powder tends to have more chocolate flavor. We use the nonalkalized type. Do not substitute an instant cocoa mix.

• Store solid chocolate, well wrapped in a cool, dark place (65°F is ideal). If storage conditions are too cold, chocolate will "sweat" when brought to room temperature. If conditions are too warm, the cocoa butter will start to melt and a gray "bloom" will form on the chocolate. This won't affect flavor or color if you melt the chocolate.

• All chocolate should be melted in a double boiler over low heat to prevent scorching. To speed melting, chop chocolate into small pieces and stir frequently. When adding liquid to melted chocolate, add at least 2 tablespoons at a time to keep the chocolate from clumping.

Equipment

Here are some basic pieces of baking equipment you will need to complete these recipes.

Mixer: A standing electric mixer with a paddle attachment is preferred, but a heavy-duty handheld mixer will suffice.

Food processor: Essential for making shortbread dough (see Scottish Shortbread, page 69, for example), some fillings (see Lattice-Top Fig and Prune Bars, page 99), batters (see Guilt-Free Spice Bars, page 72), toppings (see Almond Lattice Brownies, page 140), and crusts (see Apricot-Almond Squares, page 134). It will also make chopping nuts and other ingredients much easier.

Measuring cups and spoons: You will need two sets of measuring cups: one for dry and one for liquid. Make sure the cups for dry measure have straight rims for leveling off ingredients. Cups for liquid measure should be heat resistant, microwave safe, and have cup as well as ounce measurements.

You will also need a set of graduated metal measuring spoons for smaller amounts of both dry and liquid ingredients.

Mixing bowls: Bowls should be deep, with high sides, and heavy enough to remain stationary while you're mixing. You will also need at least one bowl that is microwave safe for melting butter and/or chocolate for some recipes (see Pecan-Caramel Brownie Cups, page 122). A nested set of Pyrex or ceramic bowls offers a variety of sizes, making it a good choice.

Spoons: Flat or concave, slotted or unslotted, wooden spoons are the right choice for mixing batters by hand. If you're mixing in a stainless-steel bowl, a wooden spoon will cut down the clatter. Choose spoons made of hardwood, such as maple; they should be smoothly finished and free of rough patches that could splinter off into your batter. Because wood is porous and absorbs odors, keep a separate set of wooden spoons just for baking.

Pots and pans: You will need heavy-bottomed saucepans for melting butter and chocolate. Most of the recipes in this book call for either a 13" by 9" rectangular baking pan or a 9- or 8-inch square baking pan. In some cases you will need a 15½" by 12" roasting pan for a water bath that will accommodate one of the other pans. You will also need a standard 12-cup muffin tin.

Spatulas: A small angled (offset) metal spatula is ideal for smoothing batter in pans and for frosting. Use a narrow metal spatula to level off dry ingredients that are being measured. To ensure that all the ingredients get mixed into the batter, you will also need a flexible rubber spatula for scraping the sides of the bowl.

Knives: A 10- to 12-inch chef's knife with a tapered blade is best for chopping, slicing, and cutting. You will also need a 2- to 3-inch paring knife for peeling and coring fruit, splitting vanilla beans, and performing other small tasks.

Whisks: Whisks come in different sizes to suit different tasks. Medium to small whisks are good for combining ingredients when you don't want to incorporate a lot of air and when you want to prevent lumps.

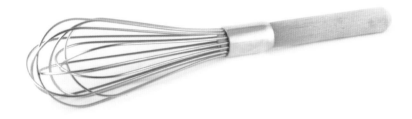

Cake tester: Some of our brownies and bars may be tested for doneness with a toothpick. Bake until a toothpick inserted 1 or 2 inches from edge comes out almost clean. With others, bake until the top or edges are lightly golden. Follow instructions in the individual recipes.

Wire racks: Good results often depend on proper cooling. Wire mesh racks with small square grids and short stubby "legs" are perfect for this purpose. They allow air to circulate underneath the pan so that the bar cookies cool evenly.

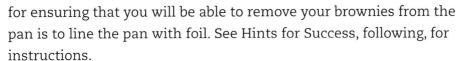

Timer: A reliable timer is a necessity for anybody who bakes. Some ovens come equipped with very accurate timers.

Aluminum foil: One of the best methods for ensuring that you will be able to remove your brownies from the pan is to line the pan with foil. See Hints for Success, following, for instructions.

Hints for Success

• Many brownie batters can be stirred with a wooden spoon, but an electric mixer makes the job easy. If your mixer is on the powerful side, you may not need to mix the batter for the full amount of time. If your model has less power, mix longer to achieve the correct consistency.

• Overmixing the batter will result in tough brownies or bars. Unless a recipe specifies otherwise, after adding flour, mix batter just until blended. Frequently scrape the side of the bowl with a rubber spatula to be sure all ingredients get mixed evenly into the batter.

• Remember to turn on the oven at least 10 to 15 minutes before baking so it has time to heat up.

• Don't rely on your oven's built-in thermometer. Use an oven thermometer (placed on the center rack in the center of the oven) to check the temperature. Before placing your pan in the oven, check and adjust the heat if necessary.

• Always use the size and shape of pan specified in the recipe (don't substitute an 8-inch for a 9-inch pan or a round for a square one and vice versa). The baking time is based on specific pan dimensions. Darker metal pans and glass pans absorb more heat than does aluminum, so check for doneness a few minutes before the time given in the recipe.

 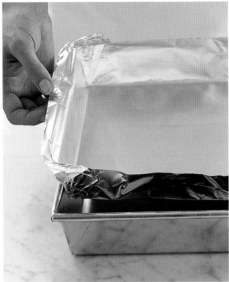

• Prepare the pan before you start mixing the batter. For easy removal of bars from pan after baking, we recommend lining the pan with foil, as shown here in the photos. To begin, turn the empty baking pan bottom side up. Cover the outside of the pan tightly with foil, shiny side out, then remove the foil cover. Use enough foil that it overlaps the edge of the pan by an inch or two. Turn the baking pan right side up and carefully fit the molded foil into it, smoothing it to fit into the edges and corners. Grease and/or dust with flour according to recipe instructions.

• Always set a kitchen timer for the shortest bake time within the range stated in the recipe to prevent overbrowning. Insert a toothpick or wooden skewer into the middle of the bar cookie to test for doneness, then cook for the longer time if necessary. Skip metal testers; crumbs don't cling to their slippery surface.

• Do not open the oven door to check on baked goods unless they are close to being done. The temperature inside the oven will drop, and baked goods may not rise properly; instead, wait until the minimum baking time is up before taking a peek.

• Be sure to cool your baked goods as directed in the recipe. Proper cooling is essential.

• To prevent jagged edges, cut bars with a chef's knife. Use a gentle sawing motion to avoid squashing the bars. For fudgy, cheesecakelike, or topped bars, dip the knife blade in hot water and quickly dry with a paper towel before each cut.

- Unless the recipe directs otherwise, store brownies and other bar cookies (cut or uncut) in the baking pan at room temperature, covered with a layer of plastic wrap or foil. You can also freeze them for up to three months. First, wrap bars in several layers of plastic wrap or foil then place them in a freezer-weight bag. If you need to pack bars for shipping or traveling, stick to recipes without dairy toppings, swirls, or sticky glazes, and wrap brownies individually.

MARBLING BROWNIE BATTER

To produce a marbled effect with two different-colored batters, pull and swirl a kitchen knife through the batters.

The Fun Begins

Baking brownies, blondies, and bar cookies can be a lot of fun, with very delicious results. They are good projects for getting kids involved in cooking, teaching them the importance of accurate measuring, the hows and whys of classic baking ingredients, ways to combine them, and maybe the hardest skill of all—patience. We hope that the information and recipes we have provided will make your baking experiences very rewarding ones.

CHOCOLATE INDULGENCES

GOOD HOUSEKEEPING'S FUDGY BROWNIES

Ultrarich, with lots of deep, dark chocolate flavor, these brownies are fabulous with or without the praline topping (see variation, opposite). For a moist, fudgy texture, do not overbake.

ACTIVE TIME: 10 MINUTES · TOTAL TIME: 40 MINUTES PLUS COOLING

MAKES: 24 BROWNIES

1¼ CUPS ALL-PURPOSE FLOUR

½ TEASPOON SALT

¾ CUP BUTTER OR MARGARINE (1½ STICKS)

4 SQUARES (4 OUNCES) UNSWEETENED CHOCOLATE, CHOPPED

4 SQUARES (4 OUNCES) SEMISWEET CHOCOLATE, CHOPPED

2 CUPS SUGAR

1 TABLESPOON VANILLA EXTRACT

5 LARGE EGGS, BEATEN

1 Preheat oven to 350°F. Line 13" by 9" baking pan with foil (see page 14); grease foil. In small bowl, with wire whisk, mix flour and salt.

2 In heavy 4-quart saucepan, melt butter and unsweetened and semisweet chocolates over low heat, stirring frequently, until smooth. Remove from heat. With wooden spoon, stir in sugar and vanilla. Add eggs; stir until well mixed. Stir flour mixture into chocolate mixture just until blended. Spread batter evenly in prepared pan.

3 Bake until toothpick inserted 1 inch from edge comes out clean, about 30 minutes. Cool completely in pan on wire rack.

4 When cool, lift foil, with brownie, out of pan; peel foil away from sides. Cut lengthwise into 4 strips, then cut each strip crosswise into 6 pieces.

EACH BROWNIE: ABOUT 206 CALORIES | 3G PROTEIN | 26G CARBOHYDRATE | 11G TOTAL FAT (6G SATURATED) | 1G FIBER | 60MG CHOLESTEROL | 121MG SODIUM

PRALINE-ICED BROWNIES

Prepare brownies as directed; cool. In 2-quart saucepan, heat **5 table-spoons butter or margarine** and **⅓ cup packed brown sugar** over medium-low heat until mixture has melted and bubbles, about 5 minutes. Remove from heat. With wire whisk, beat in **3 tablespoons bourbon or 1 tablespoon vanilla extract** plus **2 tablespoons water**; stir in **2 cups confectioners' sugar** until mixture is smooth. With small metal spatula, spread topping over room-temperature brownies; sprinkle **½ cup pecans,** toasted and coarsely chopped, over topping. Cut lengthwise into 8 strips, then cut each strip crosswise into 8 pieces. Makes 64 brownies.

EACH BROWNIE: ABOUT 297 CALORIES | 3G PROTEIN | 39G CARBOHYDRATE | 15G TOTAL FAT (8G SATURATED) | 1G FIBER | 66MG CHOLESTEROL | 147MG SODIUM

BASIC COCOA BROWNIES

Whip up these easy saucepan brownies on the spur of the moment with pantry staples.

ACTIVE TIME: 10 MINUTES · **TOTAL TIME:** 35 MINUTES PLUS COOLING
MAKES: 16 BROWNIES

½ CUP ALL-PURPOSE FLOUR

½ CUP UNSWEETENED COCOA

¼ TEASPOON BAKING POWDER

¼ TEASPOON SALT

½ CUP BUTTER OR MARGARINE (1 STICK)

1 CUP SUGAR

2 LARGE EGGS

1 TEASPOON VANILLA EXTRACT

1 CUP WALNUTS, COARSELY CHOPPED (OPTIONAL)

1 Preheat oven to 350°F. Line 9-inch square baking pan with foil (see page 14); grease foil. In small bowl, with wire whisk, mix flour, cocoa, baking powder, and salt.

2 In 3-quart saucepan, melt butter over low heat. Remove from heat and stir in sugar. Stir in eggs, one at a time, until well blended; add vanilla. Stir flour mixture into sugar mixture until blended. Stir in nuts, if using. Spread batter evenly in prepared pan.

3 Bake until toothpick inserted 2 inches from center comes out almost clean, about 25 minutes. Cool completely in pan on wire rack.

4 When cool, lift foil, with brownie, out of pan; peel foil away from sides. Cut into 4 strips, then cut each strip crosswise into 4 pieces.

EACH BROWNIE: ABOUT 132 CALORIES │ 2G PROTEIN │ 17G CARBOHYDRATE │ 7G TOTAL FAT (4G SATURATED) │ 1G FIBER │ 42MG CHOLESTEROL │ 110MG SODIUM

COCOA BROWNIES WITH MINI CHOCOLATE CHIPS

The sprinkling of miniature chocolate chips on these rich brownies is a scrumptious addition. We like to cool these treats completely before serving, because they are sometimes just too soft to cut when warm. But if the kids (and you!) are swooning from the aroma and can't wait to dig in, then go ahead and enjoy—after a brief cooling-off period. (See page 16 for photo.)

ACTIVE TIME: 15 MINUTES · TOTAL TIME: 35 MINUTES PLUS COOLING
MAKES: 16 BROWNIES

½ CUP ALL-PURPOSE FLOUR

½ CUP UNSWEETENED COCOA

¼ TEASPOON BAKING POWDER

¼ TEASPOON SALT

6 TABLESPOONS BUTTER OR MARGARINE

1 CUP SUGAR

2 LARGE EGGS

2 TEASPOONS VANILLA EXTRACT

⅓ CUP MINI CHOCOLATE CHIPS

1 Preheat oven to 350°F. Line 8-inch square baking pan with foil (see page 14); grease foil.

2 On waxed paper, combine flour, cocoa, baking powder, and salt.

3 In 3-quart saucepan, melt butter over low heat. Remove saucepan from heat; with spatula, stir in sugar, then eggs, one at a time, and vanilla until well blended. Stir in flour mixture. Spread batter in prepared pan; sprinkle with chocolate chips.

4 Bake 18 to 20 minutes or until toothpick inserted 2 inches from center comes out almost clean. Cool brownies completely in pan on wire rack, about 2 hours.

5 When cool, lift foil, with brownie, out of pan; peel foil away from sides. Cut brownies into 4 strips, then cut each strip crosswise into 4 squares.

EACH BROWNIE: ABOUT 120 CALORIES | 2G PROTEIN | 17G CARBOHYDRATE | 6G TOTAL FAT (3G SATURATED) | 1G FIBER | 36MG CHOLESTEROL | 100MG SODIUM

COCOA BROWNIES WITH BROWN BUTTER FROSTING

Did you know that baked goods made with cocoa often have a richer chocolate flavor than those made with chocolate? Here, a generous amount of cocoa—three-quarters of a cup—makes these brownies extra chocolaty.

ACTIVE TIME: 25 MINUTES · **TOTAL TIME:** 40 MINUTES PLUS COOLING
MAKES: 24 BROWNIES

BROWNIE

- 1 CUP ALL-PURPOSE FLOUR
- ¾ CUP UNSWEETENED COCOA
- ½ TEASPOON BAKING POWDER
- ½ TEASPOON SALT
- ¾ CUP BUTTER OR MARGARINE (1½ STICKS)
- 1½ CUPS GRANULATED SUGAR
- 2 TEASPOONS VANILLA EXTRACT
- 4 LARGE EGGS

BROWN BUTTER FROSTING

- 4 TABLESPOONS BUTTER (DO NOT USE MARGARINE)
- 2 CUPS CONFECTIONERS' SUGAR
- 3 TABLESPOONS MILK
- 1 TEASPOON VANILLA EXTRACT

1 Preheat oven to 350°F. Line 13" by 9" baking pan with foil (see page 14); grease foil.

2 Prepare brownie: In medium bowl, with wire whisk, mix flour, cocoa, baking powder, and salt. In 3-quart saucepan, melt butter over low heat. Remove from heat; stir in granulated sugar and vanilla. Add eggs, one at a time, stirring until well blended. Stir flour mixture into sugar mixture just until blended. Spread batter evenly in prepared pan.

3 Bake until toothpick inserted 2 inches from edge comes out almost clean, 18 to 22 minutes. Cool completely in pan on wire rack.

4 When brownie is cool, prepare frosting: In 2-quart saucepan, cook butter over medium heat, stirring occasionally, until lightly browned, 5 to 6 minutes. Remove from heat. With wooden spoon, stir in confectioners' sugar, milk, and vanilla until smooth.

5 With small metal spatula, spread frosting over cooled brownie. Lift foil, with brownie, out of pan; peel foil away from sides. Cut lengthwise into 4 strips, then cut each strip crosswise into 6 pieces.

EACH BROWNIE: ABOUT 195 CALORIES | 2G PROTEIN | 28G CARBOHYDRATE | 9G TOTAL FAT (6G SATURATED) | 1G FIBER | 58MG CHOLESTEROL | 150MG SODIUM

PENNSYLVANIA-DUTCH BROWNIES

Just a little bit of chocolate is added to these heavenly spice bars, which were inspired by the Pennsylvania-Dutch region where chocolate reigns supreme. The delicious results will make you wonder why we haven't all been doing this for years.

ACTIVE TIME: 20 MINUTES · TOTAL TIME: 35 MINUTES
MAKES: 30 BROWNIES

4   TABLESPOONS BUTTER OR MARGARINE

1   SQUARE (1 OUNCE) UNSWEETENED CHOCOLATE

¼   CUP LIGHT MOLASSES

2   LARGE EGGS

1½ CUPS ALL-PURPOSE FLOUR

1   CUP PLUS 2 TEASPOONS SUGAR

1⅛ TEASPOONS GROUND CINNAMON

1   TEASPOON GROUND GINGER

½   TEASPOON GROUND CLOVES

½   TEASPOON BAKING SODA

½   TEASPOON SALT

1   Preheat oven to 375°F. Line 13" by 9" baking pan with foil (see page 14); grease foil.

2   In 4-quart saucepan, melt butter and chocolate over low heat. Remove from heat. With wire whisk or fork, stir in molasses, then eggs. With spoon, stir in flour, 1 cup sugar, 1 teaspoon cinnamon, ginger, cloves, baking soda, and salt just until blended. Spread batter evenly in prepared pan.

3   Bake until toothpick inserted 2 inches from edge comes out clean, 15 to 20 minutes.

4   Meanwhile, in cup, combine remaining 2 teaspoons sugar and remaining ⅛ teaspoon cinnamon; set aside.

5   Remove pan from oven; immediately sprinkle brownie with cinnamon-sugar mixture. Cool in pan on wire rack at least 2 hours.

6   When cool, lift foil, with brownie, out of pan; peel foil away from sides. Cut lengthwise into 3 strips, then cut each strip crosswise into 5 pieces. Cut each piece diagonally in half.

EACH BROWNIE: ABOUT 80 CALORIES | 1G PROTEIN | 14G CARBOHYDRATE | 2G TOTAL FAT (1G SATURATED) | 0.4G FIBER | 14MG CHOLESTEROL | 80MG SODIUM

MILK CHOCOLATE–GLAZED BROWNIES

Be sure to let the brownies cool completely before preparing the milk chocolate glaze.

ACTIVE TIME: 20 MINUTES · TOTAL TIME: 50 MINUTES PLUS COOLING
MAKES: 24 BROWNIES

BROWNIE

1¼ CUPS ALL-PURPOSE FLOUR

½ TEASPOON SALT

¾ CUP BUTTER OR MARGARINE (1½ STICKS)

1 BAR (7 OUNCES) MILK CHOCOLATE

3 SQUARES (3 OUNCES) SEMISWEET CHOCOLATE

1½ CUPS SUGAR

5 LARGE EGGS

2 TEASPOONS VANILLA EXTRACT

MILK CHOCOLATE GLAZE

1 CUP MILK CHOCOLATE CHIPS (6 OUNCES)

4 TABLESPOONS BUTTER OR MARGARINE

1 TEASPOON VANILLA EXTRACT

1 Preheat oven to 350°F. Line 13" by 9" baking pan with foil (see page 14); grease foil.

2 Prepare brownie: In small bowl, with wire whisk, mix flour and salt. In 3-quart saucepan, melt butter and milk chocolate and semisweet chocolate over low heat, stirring frequently, until smooth.

3 Meanwhile, in medium bowl, with wire whisk, stir sugar, eggs, and vanilla until combined. Stir in flour mixture. Stir egg mixture into chocolate mixture until well blended. Spread batter evenly in prepared pan.

4 Bake until toothpick inserted 2 inches from edge comes out almost clean, 30 to 35 minutes. Cool completely in pan on wire rack.

5 When brownie is cool, prepare glaze: In 1-quart saucepan, melt chocolate chips and butter over low heat, stirring frequently, until smooth. Remove from heat; stir in vanilla.

6 With small metal spatula, spread glaze over cooled brownie. Lift foil, with brownie, out of pan; peel foil away from sides. Cut lengthwise into 4 strips, then cut each strip crosswise into 6 pieces.

EACH BROWNIE: ABOUT 260 CALORIES | 3G PROTEIN | 28G CARBOHYDRATE | 15G TOTAL FAT (6G SATURATED) | 1G FIBER | 70MG CHOLESTEROL | 160MG SODIUM

ROCKY ROAD BROWNIES

The original rocky road treat was a chocolate candy over which nuts and miniature marshmallows were scattered, and its name derives from its resemblance to a bumpy road. Since then, rocky road cakes, pies, tarts, and even brownies have been created—and embraced.

ACTIVE TIME: 30 MINUTES · TOTAL TIME: 55 MINUTES PLUS COOLING

MAKES: 24 BROWNIES

1¼ CUPS ALL-PURPOSE FLOUR

½ TEASPOON BAKING POWDER

½ TEASPOON SALT

¾ CUP BUTTER OR MARGARINE (1½ STICKS)

6 SQUARES (6 OUNCES) UNSWEETENED CHOCOLATE

2 CUPS SUGAR

2 TEASPOONS VANILLA EXTRACT

5 LARGE EGGS, LIGHTLY BEATEN

2 CUPS MINIATURE MARSHMALLOWS

1½ CUPS ASSORTED NUTS (6 OUNCES), TOASTED (PAGE 31) AND COARSELY CHOPPED

---

1   Preheat oven to 350°F. Line 13" by 9" baking pan with foil (see page 14); grease foil. In small bowl, with wire whisk, mix flour, baking powder, and salt.

2   In 3-quart saucepan, melt butter and chocolate over low heat, stirring frequently until smooth. Remove from heat; stir in sugar and vanilla. Add eggs; stir until well blended. Stir flour mixture into chocolate mixture just until blended. Spread batter evenly in prepared pan.

3   Bake until toothpick inserted 2 inches from edge comes out almost clean, about 20 minutes. Sprinkle top of brownie evenly with marshmallows; top with nuts. Bake until marshmallows melt slightly, about 5 minutes longer. Cool completely in pan on wire rack.

4   When cool, lift foil, with brownie, out of pan; peel foil away from sides. Cut lengthwise into 4 strips, then cut each strip crosswise into 6 pieces.

EACH BROWNIE: ABOUT 255 CALORIES | 5G PROTEIN | 29G CARBOHYDRATE | 15G TOTAL FAT (7G SATURATED) | 2G FIBER | 61MG CHOLESTEROL | 150MG SODIUM

SMALL-BATCH BROWNIES

What's changed about brownies since the 1920s? Serving size. For a guilt-free sweet treat, cut these brownies into petite squares as the original recipe directed.

ACTIVE TIME: 20 MINUTES · TOTAL TIME: 40 MINUTES PLUS COOLING
MAKES: 36 BROWNIES

½	CUP ALL-PURPOSE FLOUR	1	CUP SUGAR
¼	TEASPOON BAKING POWDER	2	LARGE EGGS
¼	TEASPOON SALT	1	TEASPOON VANILLA EXTRACT
4	TABLESPOONS BUTTER OR MARGARINE	½	CUP WALNUTS, CHOPPED
2	SQUARES (2 OUNCES) UNSWEETENED CHOCOLATE		

1 Preheat oven to 350°F. Line 9-inch square baking pan with foil (see page 14); grease foil. In small bowl, with wire whisk, mix flour, baking powder, and salt.

2 In heavy 2-quart saucepan, melt butter and chocolate over low heat, stirring frequently, until smooth. Remove from heat. Add sugar, eggs, and vanilla; whisk until blended. With wooden spoon, stir flour mixture into chocolate mixture until just blended; stir in nuts. Spread batter evenly in prepared pan.

3 Bake until toothpick inserted in center comes out almost clean, about 20 minutes. Cool completely in pan on wire rack at least 1 hour.

4 When cool, lift foil, with brownie, out of pan; peel foil away from sides. Cut into 6 strips, then cut each strip crosswise into 6 pieces.

EACH BROWNIE: ABOUT 60 CALORIES | 1G PROTEIN | 8G CARBOHYDRATE | 4G TOTAL FAT (2G SATURATED) | 0.4G FIBER | 16MG CHOLESTEROL | 36MG SODIUM

HEALTHY MAKEOVER BROWNIES

The rich texture and chocolatey goodness of these bake sale favorites speak of decadence, but compare each square's 95 calories, three grams of fat, and zero cholesterol to a regular brownie's doubly high calories, nearly quadrupled fat, and 60 milligrams of cholesterol, and you'll feel virtuous (and satisfied). Our cheats? Swapping nonfat cocoa for chocolate, and cholesterol-free spread for not-so-heart-healthy butter.

ACTIVE TIME: 15 MINUTES · TOTAL TIME: 35 MINUTES PLUS COOLING

MAKES: 16 BROWNIES

1 TEASPOON INSTANT COFFEE POWDER OR GRANULES

2 TEASPOONS VANILLA EXTRACT

½ CUP ALL-PURPOSE FLOUR

½ CUP UNSWEETENED COCOA

¼ TEASPOON BAKING POWDER

1¼ TEASPOONS SALT

1 CUP SUGAR

¼ CUP TRANS-FAT-FREE VEGETABLE OIL SPREAD (60% TO 70% OIL)

3 LARGE EGG WHITES

1 Preheat oven to 350°F. Line 8-inch square metal baking pan with foil (see page 14); grease foil. In cup, dissolve coffee in vanilla extract.

2 On waxed paper, combine flour, cocoa, baking powder, and salt.

3 In medium bowl, whisk sugar, vegetable oil spread, egg whites, and coffee mixture until well mixed; then blend in flour mixture. Spread in prepared pan.

4 Bake 22 to 24 minutes or until toothpick inserted in brownies 2 inches from edge comes out almost clean. Cool completely in pan on wire rack, about 2 hours.

5 When cool, lift foil, with brownie, out of pan; peel foil away from sides. Cut brownies into 4 strips, then cut each strip crosswise into 4 squares.

TIP If brownies are difficult to cut, dip knife in hot water; wipe dry then cut. Repeat dipping and drying as necessary.

EACH BROWNIE: ABOUT 95 CALORIES | 2G PROTEIN | 17G CARBOHYDRATE | 3G TOTAL FAT (1G SATURATED) | 1G FIBER | 0MG CHOLESTEROL | 75MG SODIUM

MALTED MILK BARS

Milkshake fans will adore these superlative bars. The frosting is made with malted milk powder and sprinkled with chopped malted milk balls.

ACTIVE TIME: 15 MINUTES · TOTAL TIME: 40 MINUTES PLUS COOLING
MAKES: 32 BARS

BROWNIE

1½ CUPS ALL-PURPOSE FLOUR

½ TEASPOON BAKING POWDER

½ TEASPOON SALT

¾ CUP BUTTER OR MARGARINE (1½ STICKS)

4 SQUARES (4 OUNCES) SEMISWEET CHOCOLATE

2 SQUARES (2 OUNCES) UNSWEETENED CHOCOLATE

1½ CUPS GRANULATED SUGAR

1 TABLESPOON VANILLA EXTRACT

4 LARGE EGGS, BEATEN

MALTED MILK TOPPING

¾ CUP MALTED MILK POWDER

3 TABLESPOONS MILK

1 TEASPOON VANILLA EXTRACT

3 TABLESPOONS BUTTER OR MARGARINE, SOFTENED

1 CUP CONFECTIONERS' SUGAR

1½ CUPS MALTED MILK BALL CANDIES (ABOUT 5 OUNCES), COARSELY CHOPPED

1 Preheat oven to 350°F. Line 13" by 9" baking pan with foil (see page 14); grease foil.

2 Prepare brownie: In small bowl, with wire whisk, mix flour, baking powder, and salt. In heavy 3-quart saucepan, melt butter and semisweet and unsweetened chocolates over low heat, stirring frequently. Remove from heat. With wooden spoon, stir in granulated sugar and vanilla. Beat in eggs until well blended. Stir in flour mixture. Spread batter in prepared pan.

3 Bake until toothpick inserted 1 inch from edge of pan comes out clean, 25 to 30 minutes. Cool completely in pan on wire rack.

4 Prepare topping: In small bowl, stir together malted milk powder, milk, and vanilla until blended. Stir in butter and confectioners' sugar until blended. With small spatula, spread topping over cooled brownie; top with chopped malted milk ball candies. Allow topping to set.

5 When topping is firm, lift foil, with brownie, out of pan; peel foil away from sides. Cut brownie lengthwise into 4 strips, then cut each strip crosswise into 8 pieces.

EACH BAR: ABOUT 200 CALORIES | 3G PROTEIN | 27G CARBOHYDRATE | 10G TOTAL FAT (5G SATURATED) | 1G FIBER | 42MG CHOLESTEROL | 155 MG SODIUM

CHOCOLATE TURTLE BROWNIES

We mounted the scrumptious components of turtle-shaped candies—pecans, caramel, and chocolate—on a sweet, golden crust.

ACTIVE TIME: 35 MINUTES · TOTAL TIME: 50 MINUTES PLUS COOLING

MAKES: 36 BARS

PASTRY CRUST

1   CUP ALL-PURPOSE FLOUR

¼   CUP GRANULATED SUGAR

⅛   TEASPOON SALT

6   TABLESPOONS COLD BUTTER, CUT INTO PIECES

3   TABLESPOONS COLD WATER

CARAMEL PECAN TOPPING

1⅓ CUPS PACKED LIGHT BROWN SUGAR

½   CUP HEAVY OR WHIPPING CREAM

⅓   CUP LIGHT CORN SYRUP

3   TABLESPOONS BUTTER

1   TEASPOON DISTILLED WHITE VINEGAR

⅛   TEASPOON SALT

1   TEASPOON VANILLA EXTRACT

¾   CUP PECANS, TOASTED (SEE OPPOSITE PAGE) AND CHOPPED

3   SQUARES (3 OUNCES) SEMISWEET CHOCOLATE

---

1   Preheat oven to 425°F. Line 9" by 9" metal baking pan with foil (see page 14); grease foil.

2   Prepare crust: In medium bowl, with wire whisk, mix flour, granulated sugar, and salt. With pastry blender or two knives used scissor-fashion, cut in butter until mixture resembles coarse crumbs. Sprinkle about 3 table-spoons cold water, 1 tablespoon at a time, into flour mixture, mixing lightly with fork after each addition until dough is just moist enough to hold together. With lightly floured hand, press dough evenly onto bottom of prepared pan. With fork, prick dough at 1-inch intervals.

3   Bake until golden (crust may crack slightly during baking), 15 to 20 minutes. Cool completely in pan on wire rack.

4   When crust is cool, prepare topping: In 2-quart saucepan, heat brown sugar, cream, corn syrup, butter, vinegar, and salt to boiling over high heat, stirring occasionally. Reduce heat to medium-low and cook, uncovered, 5 minutes, stirring frequently. Remove from heat. Stir in vanilla until mixture is blended and bubbling has subsided, about 20 seconds. Pour hot brown sugar mixture evenly over crust; sprinkle with pecans. Set aside to cool for 1 hour.

TOASTING NUTS

An easy way to make your brownies and bars taste even better is to toast the nuts, making them more flavorful.

- Preheat oven to 350°F. (If you aren't heating the oven for baking, you can use a toaster oven instead.)
- Spread out the nuts in a single layer on a rimmed baking sheet or pan; place on the middle rack in your oven.
- Heat until lightly browned, 10 to 15 minutes, stirring occasionally so nuts in the center of the pan are moved to the edges, where they will brown faster.
- Immediately transfer nuts to a cool platter or baking pan to reduce their temperature and stop browning.*
- If you're toasting just a few nuts, heat them in a dry skillet over low heat for 3 to 5 minutes, stirring frequently.

* To remove the bitter skins from hazelnuts, toast them as directed above until any portions without skin begin to brown. Transfer the nuts to a clean, dry kitchen towel and rub them until the skins come off.

5   Place chocolate in 2-cup measuring cup or medium glass bowl. In microwave oven, cook, covered with waxed paper, on High until almost melted, 1 to 2 minutes; stir until smooth. (Or, in 1-quart saucepan, heat chocolate over low heat, stirring frequently, until melted and smooth.) Cool chocolate 5 minutes; drizzle over pecans. Place pan in refrigerator until chocolate has set, about 30 minutes.

6   When set, lift foil, with pastry, out of pan; peel foil away from sides. Cut into 6 strips, then cut each strip crosswise into 6 pieces. Store bars in refrigerator.

EACH BROWNIE: ABOUT 120 CALORIES | 1G PROTEIN | 16G CARBOHYDRATE | 6G TOTAL FAT (3G SATURATED) | 1G FIBER | 12MG CHOLESTEROL | 50MG SODIUM

CARAMEL-CHOCOLATE SHORTBREAD BARS

These goodies are a cross between a cookie and a candy. Buttery shortbread is spread with gooey caramel and topped with chocolate glaze.

ACTIVE TIME: 50 MINUTES · TOTAL TIME: 1 HOUR 15 MINUTES PLUS COOLING
MAKES: 48 BARS

SHORTBREAD CRUST

¾ CUP BUTTER (1½ STICKS), SOFTENED (DO NOT USE MARGARINE)

¾ CUP CONFECTIONERS' SUGAR

1½ TEASPOONS VANILLA EXTRACT

2¼ CUPS ALL-PURPOSE FLOUR

CARAMEL FILLING

1 CUP PACKED LIGHT BROWN SUGAR

½ CUP HONEY

½ CUP BUTTER (1 STICK), CUT INTO PIECES (DO NOT USE MARGARINE)

⅓ CUP GRANULATED SUGAR

¼ CUP HEAVY OR WHIPPING CREAM

2 TEASPOONS VANILLA EXTRACT

CHOCOLATE GLAZE

3 SQUARES (3 OUNCES) SEMISWEET CHOCOLATE

1 SQUARE (1 OUNCE) UNSWEETENED CHOCOLATE

2 TABLESPOONS BUTTER (DO NOT USE MARGARINE)

1 TABLESPOON CORN SYRUP

1   Preheat oven to 350°F. Line 13" by 9" baking pan with foil (see page 14); grease foil.

2   Prepare crust: In large bowl, with mixer at medium speed, beat butter, confectioners' sugar, and vanilla until creamy, about 2 minutes. At low speed, gradually beat in flour until evenly moistened (mixture will resemble fine crumbs).

3   Sprinkle crumbs in prepared pan. With hand, firmly pat crumbs onto bottom and about ¼ inch up sides of pan to form crust. Bake until lightly browned, 25 to 30 minutes. Place on wire rack.

4   Prepare filling: In 2-quart saucepan, heat brown sugar, honey, butter, granulated sugar, cream, and vanilla, stirring frequently, to full rolling boil over high heat. Reduce heat to medium-high; set candy thermometer in place and continue cooking, without stirring, until temperature reaches 248°F, or firm-ball stage (when small amount of mixture dropped into very cold water forms a ball that does not flatten upon removal from water).

SHAPELY SHORTBREAD

Shortbread is sometimes formed using a mold to shape the dough and create raised patterns on its surface. The dough is packed into the mold, which looks like a thick wooden plate with flutings and designs carved deeply into its inner surface. Since shortbread is a Scottish specialty, you'll often see these molds decorated with a thistle motif, the national flower.

5   Pour hot caramel over warm crust. Cool in pan on wire rack 1 hour or until caramel is room temperature and has formed a skin on top.

6   Prepare glaze: In 1-quart saucepan, heat semisweet and unsweetened chocolates, butter, and corn syrup over low heat, stirring frequently, until melted and smooth.

7   Pour glaze over filling; spread evenly, being careful not to push caramel layer around. Cover and refrigerate until bars are cold and glaze has set, at least 30 minutes.

8   When cold, lift foil, with pastry, out of pan; peel foil away from sides. Cut lengthwise into 6 strips, then cut each strip crosswise into 8 bars. Store bars in refrigerator, in tightly covered container, with waxed paper between layers, up to 2 weeks.

EACH BAR: ABOUT 130 CALORIES | 1G PROTEIN | 17G CARBOHYDRATE | 7G TOTAL FAT (4G SATURATED) | 0.4G FIBER | 17MG CHOLESTEROL | 60MG SODIUM

CHOCOLATE AND PEANUT BUTTER BROWNIES

If you enjoy chocolate in your peanut butter (and the reverse), you will love these sweet, rich bars.

ACTIVE TIME: 20 MINUTES · **TOTAL TIME:** 45 MINUTES PLUS COOLING
MAKES: 24 BARS

2½ CUPS ALL-PURPOSE FLOUR	3 LARGE EGGS
1½ TEASPOONS BAKING POWDER	2 TEASPOONS VANILLA EXTRACT
½ TEASPOON SALT	3 SQUARES (3 OUNCES) SEMISWEET CHOCOLATE, MELTED
1¾ CUPS PACKED LIGHT BROWN SUGAR	
1 CUP CREAMY PEANUT BUTTER	1 SQUARE (1 OUNCE) UNSWEETENED CHOCOLATE, MELTED
½ CUP BUTTER OR MARGARINE (1 STICK), SOFTENED	1 PACKAGE (6 OUNCES) SEMISWEET CHOCOLATE CHIPS (1 CUP)

1   Preheat oven to 350°F. Line 13" by 9" baking pan with foil (see page 14); do not grease foil. In medium bowl, with wire whisk, mix flour, baking powder, and salt.

2   In large bowl, with mixer at medium speed, beat brown sugar, peanut butter, and butter until smooth, about 2 minutes. Reduce speed to low. Add eggs and vanilla; beat until smooth. Beat in flour mixture just until combined (dough will be stiff).

3   Place one-third of dough (about 1¾ cups) in another large bowl. Stir in melted semisweet and unsweetened chocolates until blended. Fold in ¼ cup semisweet chocolate pieces.

4   Pat half of remaining peanut-butter dough into prepared baking pan. In random pattern, drop chocolate dough and remaining peanut-butter dough on top of peanut-butter layer; pat down with hand. Sprinkle with remaining chocolate pieces.

5   Bake until toothpick inserted in center comes out clean, 25 to 30 minutes. Cool in pan on rack.

6   When cool, lift foil, with brownie, out of pan; peel foil away from sides. Cut lengthwise into 4 strips, then cut each strip crosswise into 6 pieces.

EACH BROWNIE: ABOUT 270 CALORIES | 5G PROTEIN | 36G CARBOHYDRATE | 13G TOTAL FAT (4G SATURATED) | 2G FIBER | 37MG CHOLESTEROL | 178MG SODIUM

RASPBERRY BROWNIES

Raspberries and chocolate are a lovely combination. We suggest using seedless raspberry jam, but if you have raspberry jam with seeds in your pantry, press it through a coarse sieve to remove the seeds.

ACTIVE TIME: 20 MINUTES · **TOTAL TIME:** 50 MINUTES PLUS COOLING
MAKES: 36 BROWNIES

---

1 CUP ALL-PURPOSE FLOUR	1½ CUPS SUGAR
¾ CUP UNSWEETENED COCOA	4 LARGE EGGS
½ TEASPOON BAKING POWDER	¾ CUP SEEDLESS RASPBERRY JAM
½ TEASPOON SALT	2 TEASPOONS VANILLA EXTRACT
1 CUP BUTTER OR MARGARINE (2 STICKS)	

1   Preheat oven to 350°F. Line 13" by 9" baking pan with foil (see page 14); grease foil. In small bowl, with wire whisk, mix flour, cocoa, baking powder, and salt.

2   In 3-quart saucepan, melt butter over low heat. Remove from heat. With wire whisk, stir in sugar. Add eggs, one at a time, beating well after each addition. Stir in jam and vanilla, whisking until well mixed. With wooden spoon, stir flour mixture into butter mixture just until blended. Spread batter evenly in prepared pan.

3   Bake until toothpick inserted 2 inches from edge comes out almost clean, 30 to 35 minutes. Cool completely in pan on wire rack.

4   When cool, lift foil, with brownie, out of pan; peel foil away from sides. Cut lengthwise into 6 strips, then cut each strip crosswise into 6 pieces.

EACH BROWNIE: ABOUT 125 CALORIES | 2G PROTEIN | 16G CARBOHYDRATE | 6G TOTAL FAT (4G SATURATED) | 1G FIBER | 38MG CHOLESTEROL | 105MG SODIUM

EASY RASPBERRY BROWNIES

If you have a box of brownie mix and a jar of raspberry jam you are well on your way to creating these irresistible treats.

ACTIVE TIME: 10 MINUTES · **TOTAL TIME:** 40 MINUTES PLUS COOLING
MAKES: 36 BROWNIES

1   BOX (19½ TO 22½ OUNCES)
      FAMILY-SIZE 13"X9" BROWNIE MIX

¾   CUP SEEDLESS RASPBERRY JAM

1   Preheat oven to 350°F. Line 13" by 9" baking pan with foil (see page 14); grease foil.
2   Prepare brownie mix according to package directions. Stir in jam until well blended. Spread batter evenly in prepared pan.
3   Bake until toothpick inserted 2 inches from edge comes out almost clean, 30 to 35 minutes. Cool completely in pan on wire rack.
4   When cool, lift foil, with brownie, out of pan; peel foil away from sides. Cut lengthwise into 6 strips, then cut each strip crosswise into 6 pieces.

EACH BROWNIE: ABOUT 114 CALORIES | 1G PROTEIN | 18G CARBOHYDRATE | 5G TOTAL FAT (1G SATURATED) | 1G FIBER | 12MG CHOLESTEROL | 71MG SODIUM

BLACK FOREST BROWNIES

Kirsch, sour cherries, and chocolate are the hallmarks of Black Forest cake, which was originally created in the Black Forest region of Germany. We've captured all the fabulous flavor of the classic in a brownie that takes twenty minutes to prepare.

ACTIVE TIME: 20 MINUTES · TOTAL TIME: 45 MINUTES PLUS COOLING

MAKES: 24 BROWNIES

---

1   CUP ALL-PURPOSE FLOUR

½   TEASPOON SALT

¾   CUP BUTTER OR MARGARINE (1½ STICKS)

½   CUP UNSWEETENED COCOA

2   TABLESPOONS KIRSCH (CHERRY BRANDY), OPTIONAL

1¾ CUPS SUGAR

3   TEASPOONS VANILLA EXTRACT

4   LARGE EGGS, LIGHTLY BEATEN

¾   CUP DRIED TART CHERRIES

1   CONTAINER (16 OUNCES) SOUR CREAM

1   Preheat oven to 350°F. Line 13" by 9" baking pan with foil (see page 14); grease foil. In small bowl, with wire whisk, mix flour and salt.

2   In 3-quart saucepan, melt butter over low heat. Remove from heat. With wire whisk, stir in cocoa until smooth. Add kirsch, if using, 1½ cups sugar, and 2 teaspoons vanilla; whisk until well mixed. Add eggs; stir until well combined. Stir flour mixture into cocoa mixture just until blended; stir in cherries. Spread batter evenly in prepared pan.

3   Bake until toothpick inserted 1 inch from edge comes out almost clean, 20 to 25 minutes.

4   Meanwhile, in small bowl, stir sour cream, remaining ¼ cup sugar, and remaining 1 teaspoon vanilla until blended. With small metal spatula, spread sour cream mixture evenly over baked brownie. Return to oven and continue baking until topping has set, about 5 minutes longer. Cool completely in pan on wire rack.

5   When cool, lift foil, with brownie, out of pan; peel foil away from sides. Cut lengthwise into 4 strips, then cut each strip crosswise into 6 pieces.

EACH BROWNIE: ABOUT 200 CALORIES | 3G PROTEIN | 23G CARBOHYDRATE | 11G TOTAL FAT (7G SATURATED) | 2G FIBER | 60MG CHOLESTEROL | 130MG SODIUM

EASY BLACK FOREST BROWNIES

Sour cream and tart dried cherries are the secret ingredients in these brownies.

ACTIVE TIME: 15 MINUTES · **TOTAL TIME:** 40 MINUTES PLUS COOLING

MAKES: 24 BROWNIES

---

1   BOX (19½ TO 22½ OUNCES) FAMILY-SIZE 13"X9" BROWNIE MIX

¾   CUP TART DRIED CHERRIES

1   CONTAINER (16 OUNCES) SOUR CREAM

¼   CUP SUGAR

1   TEASPOON VANILLA EXTRACT

1   Preheat oven to 350°F. Line 13" by 9" baking pan with foil (see page 14); grease foil.

2   Prepare brownie mix according to package directions. Stir in cherries. Spread batter evenly in prepared pan.

3   Bake until toothpick inserted 1 inch from edge comes out almost clean, 20 to 25 minutes.

4   Meanwhile, in small bowl, stir sour cream, sugar, and vanilla until blended. With small metal spatula, spread sour cream mixture evenly over baked brownie. Return to oven and continue baking until topping is set, about 5 minutes longer. Cool completely in pan on wire rack.

5   When cool, lift foil, with brownie, out of pan; peel foil away from sides. Cut lengthwise into 4 strips, then cut each strip crosswise into 6 pieces.

EACH BROWNIE: ABOUT 207 CALORIES | 3G PROTEIN | 2G CARBOHYDRATE | 11G TOTAL FAT (4G SATURATED) | 2G FIBER | 26MG CHOLESTEROL | 113MG SODIUM

GOOEY CHEESECAKE BROWNIES

These brownies have two layers: a deep chocolate base and a sweet cream-cheese topping that is spread over the brownie base before baking. For easy cutting, lightly spray the knife with cooking spray or dip it into hot water, then shake off the excess.

ACTIVE TIME: 25 MINUTES · **TOTAL TIME:** 1 HOUR 20 MINUTES PLUS COOLING
MAKES: 36 BROWNIES

BROWNIE

1¼ CUPS ALL-PURPOSE FLOUR

½   TEASPOON SALT

¾   CUP BUTTER OR MARGARINE (1½ STICKS)

6   SQUARES (6 OUNCES) UNSWEETENED CHOCOLATE

2   CUPS GRANULATED SUGAR

1   TEASPOON VANILLA EXTRACT

3   LARGE EGGS, LIGHTLY BEATEN

GOOEY TOPPING

1   PACKAGE (8 OUNCES) CREAM CHEESE, SOFTENED

2   LARGE EGGS

2   CUPS CONFECTIONERS' SUGAR

1   TEASPOON VANILLA EXTRACT

1   Preheat oven to 350°F. Line 13" by 9" baking pan with foil (see page 14); grease foil.

2   Prepare brownie: In small bowl, with wire whisk, mix flour and salt. In 3-quart saucepan, melt butter and chocolate over low heat, stirring frequently, until smooth. Remove from heat; stir in granulated sugar and vanilla. Add eggs; stir until well blended. Stir flour mixture into chocolate mixture just until blended. Spread batter evenly in prepared pan.

3   Prepare topping: In medium bowl, with mixer at low speed, beat cream cheese, eggs, confectioners' sugar, and vanilla until well combined. With small metal spatula, gently spread topping over batter.

4   Bake until toothpick inserted 2 inches from edge comes out almost clean and top turns golden brown, 55 to 60 minutes. Cool completely in pan on wire rack.

5   When cool, lift foil, with brownie, out of pan; peel foil away from sides. Cut lengthwise into 6 strips, then cut each strip crosswise into 6 pieces.

EACH BROWNIE: ABOUT 175 CALORIES | 3G PROTEIN | 22G CARBOHYDRATE | 9G TOTAL FAT (6G SATURATED) | 1G FIBER | 47MG CHOLESTEROL | 100MG SODIUM

GERMAN CHOCOLATE BROWNIES

These brownies boast a chocolate base made with sweetened baking chocolate and a caramel and coconut-pecan frosting, just like their namesake. But the beauty is, you can whip up the batter in a single pan and the frosting in one bowl for a finished dessert in a jiffy.

ACTIVE TIME: 25 MINUTES · TOTAL TIME: I HOUR 10 MINUTES PLUS COOLING

MAKES: 36 BROWNIES

BROWNIE

½ CUP BUTTER OR MARGARINE (1 STICK)

2 PACKAGES (4 OUNCES EACH) SWEET BAKING CHOCOLATE

1 CUP PACKED BROWN SUGAR

3 LARGE EGGS, LIGHTLY BEATEN

1 TEASPOON VANILLA EXTRACT

1 CUP ALL-PURPOSE FLOUR

½ TEASPOON SALT

GERMAN CHOCOLATE TOPPING

3 LARGE EGG WHITES

2 CUPS SWEETENED FLAKED COCONUT

1 CUP PECANS, TOASTED (PAGE 31) AND CHOPPED

½ CUP PACKED BROWN SUGAR

¼ CUP WHOLE MILK

½ TEASPOON VANILLA EXTRACT

⅛ TEASPOON ALMOND EXTRACT

⅛ TEASPOON SALT

1 Preheat oven to 350°F. Line 13" by 9" baking pan with foil (see page 14); grease foil.

2 Prepare brownie: In 3-quart saucepan, heat butter and chocolate over medium-low heat until melted, stirring frequently. Remove saucepan from heat; stir in brown sugar. Add eggs and vanilla; stir until well mixed. Stir in flour and salt just until blended. Spread batter evenly in prepared pan.

3 Prepare topping: In medium bowl, with wire whisk, beat egg whites until foamy. Stir in coconut, pecans, brown sugar, milk, vanilla and almond extracts, and salt until well combined. Spread topping over batter.

4 Bake until toothpick inserted 2 inches from edge comes out almost clean and topping turns golden brown, 45 to 50 minutes. Cool completely in pan on wire rack.

5 When cool, lift foil, with brownie, out of pan; peel foil away from sides. Cut lengthwise into 6 strips, then cut each strip crosswise into 6 pieces.

EACH BROWNIE: ABOUT 150 CALORIES | 2G PROTEIN | 18G CARBOHYDRATE | 8G TOTAL FAT (4G SATURATED) | 2G FIBER | 25MG CHOLESTEROL | 85MG SODIUM

EASY GERMAN CHOCOLATE BROWNIES

As if our German Chocolate Brownies at left weren't easy enough to make, we've further simplified the recipe by substituting brownie mix from a box. The results are equally sweet, and leave you with a little extra time we're sure you'll know how to use.

ACTIVE TIME: 15 MINUTES · TOTAL TIME: 55 MINUTES PLUS COOLING
MAKES: 36 BROWNIES

1   BOX (19½ TO 22½ OUNCES) FAMILY-SIZE 13"X9" BROWNIE MIX

3   LARGE EGG WHITES

2   CUPS SWEETENED FLAKED COCONUT

1   CUP PECANS, TOASTED (PAGE 31) AND CHOPPED

½   CUP PACKED BROWN SUGAR

½   TEASPOON VANILLA EXTRACT

⅛   TEASPOON ALMOND EXTRACT

⅛   TEASPOON SALT

1   Preheat oven to 350°F. Line 13" by 9" baking pan with foil (see page 14); grease foil.

2   Prepare brownie mix according to package directions. Spread batter evenly in prepared pan. Bake brownie 20 minutes.

3   Meanwhile, in medium bowl, with wire whisk, beat egg whites until foamy. Stir in coconut, pecans, sugar, vanilla and almond extracts, and salt until well combined. Spoon topping over hot brownie and spread evenly.

4   Return brownie to oven and bake until toothpick inserted 2 inches from edge comes out almost clean, 20 to 25 minutes longer. Cool completely in pan on wire rack.

5   When cool, lift foil, with brownie, out of pan; peel foil away from sides. Cut lengthwise into 6 strips, then cut each strip crosswise into 6 pieces.

EACH BROWNIE: ABOUT 151 CALORIES | 2G PROTEIN | 19G CARBOHYDRATE | 8G TOTAL FAT (2G SATURATED) | 1G FIBER | 12MG CHOLESTEROL | 93MG SODIUM

MISSISSIPPI MUD BARS

Dense as mud, rich as a millionaire—and they freeze well. Don't tell anyone, but these bars taste great frozen.

ACTIVE TIME: 20 MINUTES · TOTAL TIME: 55 MINUTES PLUS COOLING
MAKES: 32 BARS

MUD CAKE

- ¾ CUP BUTTER OR MARGARINE (1½ STICKS)
- 1¾ CUPS GRANULATED SUGAR
- ¾ CUP UNSWEETENED COCOA
- 4 LARGE EGGS, LIGHTLY BEATEN
- 2 TEASPOONS VANILLA EXTRACT
- ½ TEASPOON SALT
- 1½ CUPS ALL-PURPOSE FLOUR
- ½ CUP PECANS, CHOPPED
- ½ CUP FLAKED SWEETENED COCONUT
- 3 CUPS MINIATURE MARSHMALLOWS

FUDGE TOPPING

- 5 TABLESPOONS BUTTER OR MARGARINE
- 1 SQUARE (1 OUNCE) UNSWEETENED CHOCOLATE, CHOPPED
- ⅓ CUP UNSWEETENED COCOA
- ⅛ TEASPOON SALT
- ¼ CUP EVAPORATED MILK (NOT SWEETENED CONDENSED MILK) OR HEAVY OR WHIPPING CREAM
- 1 TEASPOON VANILLA EXTRACT
- 1 CUP CONFECTIONERS' SUGAR
- ½ CUP PECANS, COARSELY BROKEN
- ¼ CUP FLAKED SWEETENED COCONUT

1 Preheat oven to 350°F. Line 13" by 9" baking pan with foil (see page 14); grease and flour foil.

2 Prepare cake: In 3-quart saucepan, melt butter over low heat. With wire whisk, stir in granulated sugar and cocoa. Remove from heat. Beat in eggs, one at a time. Beat in vanilla and salt until well blended. With wooden spoon, stir in flour just until blended, then stir in pecans and coconut. Spread batter in prepared pan (batter will be thick).

3 Bake 25 minutes. Remove from oven. Sprinkle marshmallows in even layer on top of cake. Return to oven and bake until marshmallows are puffed and golden, about 10 minutes longer. Cool completely in pan on wire rack.

4 When cake is cool, prepare topping: In heavy 2-quart saucepan, melt butter and chocolate over low heat, stirring frequently, until smooth. With wire whisk, stir in cocoa and salt until smooth. Stir in evaporated milk and vanilla (mixture will be thick). Beat in confectioners' sugar until smooth and blended. Pour hot topping over cake. Cool 20 minutes.

5 When cool, sprinkle pecans and coconut over top. Serve at room temperature or chilled. To serve, lift foil, with brownie, out of pan; peel foil away from sides. Cut lengthwise into 4 strips, then cut each strip crosswise into 8 pieces.

EACH BAR: ABOUT 204 CALORIES | 3G PROTEIN | 26G CARBOHYDRATE | 11G TOTAL FAT (5G SATURATED) | 2G FIBER | 44MG CHOLESTEROL | 125MG SODIUM

EASY MISSISSIPPI MUD BARS

Who knew you could make mud cake from a box of brownie mix?

ACTIVE TIME: 15 MINUTES · TOTAL TIME: 45 MINUTES PLUS COOLING
MAKES: 32 BARS

MUD CAKE

- 1 BOX (19½ TO 22½ OUNCES) FAMILY-SIZE 13"X9" BROWNIE MIX
- ½ CUP PECANS, CHOPPED
- ½ CUP SWEETENED FLAKED COCONUT
- 3 CUPS MINIATURE MARSHMALLOWS

FUDGE TOPPING

- 5 TABLESPOONS BUTTER OR MARGARINE
- 1 SQUARE (1 OUNCE) UNSWEETENED CHOCOLATE, CHOPPED
- ⅓ CUP UNSWEETENED COCOA
- ⅛ TEASPOON SALT
- ¼ CUP EVAPORATED MILK (NOT SWEETENED CONDENSED MILK) OR HEAVY OR WHIPPING CREAM
- 1 TEASPOON VANILLA EXTRACT
- 1 CUP CONFECTIONERS' SUGAR
- ½ CUP PECANS, COARSELY BROKEN
- ¼ CUP SWEETENED FLAKED COCONUT

1 Preheat oven to 350°F. Line 13" by 9" baking pan with foil (see page 14); grease and flour foil.

2 Prepare cake: Prepare brownie mix according to package directions. Stir in pecans and coconut. Spread batter evenly in prepared pan. Bake until toothpick inserted 2 inches from edge comes out almost clean, 20 to 25 minutes. Sprinkle marshmallows evenly on hot cake. Bake until marshmallows are puffed and golden, 10 minutes. Cool completely in pan on wire rack.

3 Prepare topping: In heavy 2-quart saucepan, melt butter and chocolate over low heat, stirring frequently, until smooth. With wire whisk, stir in cocoa and salt until smooth. Stir in evaporated milk and vanilla. Beat in confectioners' sugar until smooth and blended. Pour hot topping over cake. Cool 20 minutes.

4 When cool, sprinkle pecans and coconut over top. Serve at room temperature or chilled. To serve, lift foil, with brownie, out of pan; peel foil away from sides. Cut lengthwise into 4 strips, then cut each strip crosswise into 8 pieces.

EACH BAR: ABOUT 196 CALORIES | 2G PROTEIN | 25G CARBOHYDRATE | 11G TOTAL FAT (3G SATURATED) | 2G FIBER | 19MG CHOLESTEROL | 114MG SODIUM

S'MORE BARS

Kids at summer camp toast marshmallows over a campfire to make these chocolatey cookie treats. Now you can make them at home any time of the year. We included graham crackers in both the batter and topping to give the recipe the flavor of the original.

ACTIVE TIME: 15 MINUTES · **TOTAL TIME:** 55 MINUTES PLUS COOLING
MAKES: 24 BARS

8 GRAHAM CRACKERS (5" BY 2½" EACH)
1½ CUPS ALL-PURPOSE FLOUR
2¼ TEASPOONS BAKING POWDER
1 TEASPOON SALT
¾ CUP BUTTER OR MARGARINE (1½ STICKS), SOFTENED
1 CUP PACKED LIGHT BROWN SUGAR
¾ CUP GRANULATED SUGAR
1 TABLESPOON VANILLA EXTRACT
4 LARGE EGGS
1 CUP WALNUTS OR PECANS, COARSELY CHOPPED
1 BAR (7 TO 8 OUNCES) SEMISWEET OR MILK CHOCOLATE, CUT INTO SMALL PIECES
2 CUPS MINIATURE MARSHMALLOWS

1 Preheat oven to 350°F. Line 13" by 9" baking pan with foil (see page 14); grease and flour foil.

2 Coarsely crumble enough graham crackers to equal 1 cup pieces; set aside. With rolling pin, crush remaining graham crackers to equal ½ cup fine crumbs.

3 In medium bowl, with wire whisk, mix flour, baking powder, salt, and finely crushed graham-cracker crumbs.

4 In heavy 3-quart saucepan, melt butter over low heat. Remove from heat. With wooden spoon, stir in light brown and granulated sugars and vanilla, then stir in eggs one at time until well blended. Add flour mixture and stir just until blended. Stir in chopped nuts. Spread batter evenly in prepared pan.

5 Bake until top is lightly golden, 30 minutes. Remove from oven. Sprinkle with graham-cracker pieces, chocolate-bar pieces, and marshmallows. Return to oven and bake until marshmallows are puffed and golden, 10 minutes longer. Cool completely in pan on wire rack.

6 When cool, lift foil, with brownie, out of pan; peel foil away from sides. Cut lengthwise into 4 strips, then cut each strip crosswise into 6 pieces.

EACH BAR: ABOUT 260 CALORIES | 3G PROTEIN | 36G CARBOHYDRATE | 12G TOTAL FAT (2G SATURATED) | 1G FIBER | 36MG CHOLESTEROL | 250MG SODIUM

MINT-CHOCOLATE BROWNIES

A double dose of mint makes these brownies a winner: The batter is laden with mint-chocolate candies, and the icing has a touch of mint liqueur.

ACTIVE TIME: 25 MINUTES · TOTAL TIME: 50 MINUTES PLUS COOLING
MAKES: 24 BROWNIES

BROWNIE

1¼ CUPS ALL-PURPOSE FLOUR

½   TEASPOON SALT

¾   CUP BUTTER OR MARGARINE (1½ STICKS)

4   SQUARES (4 OUNCES) SEMISWEET CHOCOLATE

4   SQUARES (4 OUNCES) UNSWEETENED CHOCOLATE

2   CUPS SUGAR

1   TABLESPOON VANILLA EXTRACT

5   LARGE EGGS, LIGHTLY BEATEN

1   PACKAGE (4 TO 5 OUNCES) CHOCOLATE AND MINT–LAYERED CANDIES (ABOUT 1 CUP), EACH BROKEN IN HALF

MINT-CHOCOLATE ICING

1   PACKAGE (6 OUNCES) SEMISWEET CHOCOLATE CHIPS (1 CUP)

4   TABLESPOONS BUTTER OR MARGARINE

1   TABLESPOON CRÈME DE MENTHE

1   Preheat oven to 350°F. Line 13" by 9" baking pan with foil (see page 14); grease foil.

2   Prepare brownie: In small bowl, with wire whisk, mix flour and salt. In 3-quart saucepan, melt butter and chocolates over low heat, stirring often, until smooth. Remove from heat; stir in sugar and vanilla. Add eggs; stir until well mixed. Stir in candies. Stir flour mixture into chocolate mixture just until blended. Spread batter evenly in prepared pan.

3   Bake until toothpick inserted 2 inches from edge comes out almost clean, 25 to 30 minutes. Cool completely in pan on wire rack.

4   When brownie is cool, prepare icing: In small microwave-safe bowl, heat chocolate and butter on High 30 seconds; stir in crème de menthe until well blended. If chocolate isn't completely melted, microwave on High 5 to 10 seconds; stir until smooth.

5   With small spatula, spread icing over cooled brownie. Allow icing to set. Lift foil, with brownie, out of pan; peel foil away from sides. Cut lengthwise into 4 strips, then cut each strip crosswise into 6 pieces.

EACH BROWNIE: ABOUT 280 CALORIES | 4G PROTEIN | 34G CARBOHYDRATE | 16G TOTAL FAT (10G SATURATED) | 2G FIBER | 66MG CHOLESTEROL | 145MG SODIUM

EASY MINT-CHOCOLATE BROWNIES

These brownies require just a few ingredients. Why not keep them on hand so you can whip up these double-mint brownies anytime?

ACTIVE TIME: 20 MINUTES · **TOTAL TIME:** 45 MINUTES PLUS COOLING
MAKES: 24 BROWNIES

1 BOX (19½ TO 22½ OUNCES) FAMILY-STYLE 13"X9" BROWNIE MIX

1 PACKAGE (4 TO 5 OUNCES) CHOCOLATE AND MINT-LAYERED CANDIES (ABOUT 1 CUP), EACH BROKEN IN HALF

1 PACKAGE (6 OUNCES) SEMISWEET CHOCOLATE CHIPS (1 CUP)

4 TABLESPOONS BUTTER OR MARGARINE

1 TABLESPOON CRÈME DE MENTHE

1 Preheat oven to 350°F. Line 13" by 9" baking pan with foil (see page 14); grease foil.

2 Prepare brownie mix according to package directions. Stir in mint candies. Spread batter evenly in prepared pan.

3 Bake until toothpick inserted 2 inches from edge comes out almost clean, 25 to 30 minutes. Cool in pan on wire rack.

4 In small microwave-safe bowl, heat chocolate and butter on High 30 seconds. Stir in crème de menthe until smooth and well blended. If chocolate isn't completely melted, microwave on High 5 to 10 seconds; stir until smooth.

5 With small spatula, spread icing over cooled brownie. Allow icing to set. Lift foil, with brownie, out of pan; peel foil away from sides. Cut lengthwise into 4 strips, then cut each strip crosswise into 6 pieces.

EACH BROWNIE: ABOUT 230 CALORIES | 3G PROTEIN | 28G CARBOHYDRATE | 13G TOTAL FAT (5G SATURATED) | 1G FIBER | 23MG CHOLESTEROL | 126MG SODIUM

BROWNIE SUNDAE CUPS

What's not to love about a brownie "muffin" stuffed with ice cream and drizzled with hot fudge sauce? We provide a recipe for homemade fudge topping, but you can take a shortcut and use store-bought if you prefer.

ACTIVE TIME: 20 MINUTES · TOTAL TIME: 30 MINUTES PLUS COOLING
MAKES: 6 SERVINGS

BROWNIE CUPS

1	CUP ALL-PURPOSE FLOUR
½	CUP UNSWEETENED COCOA
1	TEASPOON BAKING POWDER
¼	TEASPOON SALT
¾	CUP BUTTER OR MARGARINE (1½ STICKS)
1½	CUPS SUGAR
3	LARGE EGGS, LIGHTLY BEATEN
2	TEASPOONS VANILLA EXTRACT

HOT FUDGE SAUCE

½	CUP SUGAR
⅓	CUP UNSWEETENED COCOA
¼	CUP HEAVY OR WHIPPING CREAM
2	TABLESPOONS BUTTER OR MARGARINE
1	TEASPOON VANILLA EXTRACT
1	PINT VANILLA ICE CREAM

1   Preheat oven to 350°F. Grease 6 jumbo muffin-pan cups (about 4" by 2" each) or six 6-ounce custard cups.

2   Prepare cups: In small bowl, with wire whisk, mix flour, cocoa, baking powder, and salt. In 3-quart saucepan, melt butter over medium-low heat. Remove from heat; stir in sugar. Add eggs and vanilla; stir until well mixed. Stir in flour mixture just until blended. Spoon batter evenly into cups.

3   Bake until toothpick inserted in center comes out almost clean, 30 to 35 minutes. Cool in pan on wire rack 5 minutes. Run tip of thin knife around edge of each brownie to loosen. Invert onto rack and cool 10 minutes longer to serve warm, or cool completely to serve later.

4   While brownie cups are cooling, prepare sauce: In heavy 1-quart saucepan, heat sugar, cocoa, cream, and butter to boiling over medium-high heat, stirring frequently. Remove from heat; stir in vanilla. Serve sauce warm, or cool completely, then cover and refrigerate for up to 2 weeks. Gently reheat before using. (Makes about ⅔ cup.)

5   Assemble sundaes: With small knife, cut 1½- to 2-inch circle in center of each brownie; remove top and set aside. Scoop out brownie centers, making sure not to scoop through bottom. Transfer centers to small bowl and reserve to sprinkle over ice cream another day. Place each brownie cup on dessert plate. Scoop ice cream into brownie cups and drizzle with hot fudge sauce; replace brownie tops.

EACH SERVING WITHOUT SAUCE: ABOUT 500 CALORIES | 7G PROTEIN | 61G CARBOHYDRATE 28G TOTAL FAT (16G SATURATED) | 2G FIBER | 152MG CHOLESTEROL | 355MG SODIUM

EACH TABLESPOON SAUCE: ABOUT 80 CALORIES | 1G PROTEIN | 10G CARBOHYDRATE 5G TOTAL FAT (3G SATURATED) | 1G FIBER | 14MG CHOLESTEROL | 25MG SODIUM

PATCHWORK BROWNIES

The patchwork pattern is easy to achieve—random drops of light batter are filled in by drops of dark batter—but everyone will be impressed nonetheless.

ACTIVE TIME: 25 MINUTES · **TOTAL TIME:** 55 MINUTES PLUS COOLING
MAKES: 24 BROWNIES

---

2   CUPS ALL-PURPOSE FLOUR

1   TEASPOON BAKING POWDER

¼   TEASPOON SALT

1¼ CUPS PACKED BROWN SUGAR

1   CUP BUTTER OR MARGARINE (2 STICKS), SOFTENED

4   LARGE EGGS

1½ TEASPOONS VANILLA EXTRACT

1   CUP PECANS, TOASTED (PAGE 31) AND CHOPPED

¾   CUP SEMISWEET CHOCOLATE CHIPS

4   SQUARES (4 OUNCES) UNSWEETENED CHOCOLATE, MELTED

½   CUP GRANULATED SUGAR

¾   CUP WHITE CHOCOLATE CHIPS

1   Preheat oven to 350°F. Line 13" by 9" baking pan with foil (see page 14); grease foil. In medium bowl, with wire whisk, mix flour, baking powder, and salt.

2   In large bowl, with mixer at low speed, beat brown sugar and butter until creamy, about 2 minutes. Beat in 3 eggs, one at a time, beating well after each addition; beat in vanilla. Add flour mixture; beat just until blended, occasionally scraping bowl with rubber spatula. With spoon, stir in pecans.

3   Transfer 2 cups batter to medium bowl; stir in semisweet chocolate chips. To batter remaining in large bowl (this should be about 1½ cups), add melted chocolate, granulated sugar, and remaining egg; stir well until blended. With spoon, stir in white chocolate chips.

4   Randomly drop light batter by heaping teaspoons about 1 inch apart into prepared pan. Drop dark batter into empty spaces.

5   Bake until toothpick inserted in center comes out almost clean, 30 to 35 minutes. Cool completely in pan on wire rack.

6   When cool, lift foil, with brownie, out of pan; peel foil away from sides. Cut lengthwise into 4 strips, then cut each strip crosswise into 6 pieces.

EACH BROWNIE: ABOUT 295 CALORIES | 4G PROTEIN | 32G CARBOHYDRATE | 18G TOTAL FAT (9G SATURATED) | 2G FIBER | 58MG CHOLESTEROL | 145MG SODIUM

EASY PATCHWORK BROWNIES

Boxed brownie mix simplifies the process without compromising the impressive patchwork effect.

ACTIVE TIME: 20 MINUTES · TOTAL TIME: 50 MINUTES

MAKES: 24 BROWNIES

1   BOX (19½ TO 22½ OUNCES) FAMILY-SIZE 13"X9" BROWNIE MIX

5   TABLESPOONS BUTTER OR MARGARINE

½   CUP PACKED BROWN SUGAR

1   LARGE EGG

½   TEASPOON VANILLA EXTRACT

½   CUP ALL-PURPOSE FLOUR

½   TEASPOON BAKING POWDER

½   CUP PECANS OR WALNUTS, CHOPPED

1   Preheat oven to 350°F. Line 13" by 9" baking pan with foil (see page 14); grease foil.

2   Prepare brownie mix according to package directions. Spread 1½ cups batter evenly in prepared pan.

3   To make blondie batter: In small saucepan, melt butter over low heat. Remove from heat and stir in brown sugar. Add egg and vanilla; stir until well blended. Add flour, baking powder, and pecans; stir until blended.

4   Spoon remaining brownie batter and blondie batter by alternating heaping teaspoonsful over batter in pan.

5   Bake until toothpick inserted 2 inches from edge of pan comes out almost clean, 30 to 35 minutes. Cool completely in pan on wire rack.

6   When cool, lift foil, with brownie, out of pan; peel foil away from sides. Cut lengthwise into 4 strips, then cut each strip crosswise into 6 pieces.

EACH BROWNIE: ABOUT 213 CALORIES | 3G PROTEIN | 27G CARBOHYDRATE | 11G TOTAL FAT (3G SATURATED) | 1G FIBER | 33MG CHOLESTEROL | 142MG SODIUM

LAYERED MOCHA BARS

A graham cracker crust is sprinkled with chocolate chips, coconut, and pecans then blanketed with a layer of espresso-flavored sweetened condensed milk.

ACTIVE TIME: 25 MINUTES · TOTAL TIME: 45 MINUTES PLUS COOLING AND CHILLING
MAKES: 48 BARS

½ CUP BUTTER OR MARGARINE (1 STICK)

1 BAG (7 OUNCES) SWEETENED FLAKED COCONUT

1 PACKAGE (8 OUNCES) CHOPPED PECANS

12 CHOCOLATE GRAHAM CRACKERS (5" BY 2½" EACH)

1 TABLESPOON INSTANT COFFEE OR ESPRESSO-COFFEE POWDER

1 TABLESPOON VERY HOT WATER

1 CAN (14 OUNCES) SWEETENED CONDENSED MILK

1 PACKAGE (12 OUNCES) SEMISWEET CHOCOLATE CHIPS (2 CUPS)

1 Preheat oven to 350°F. Line 13" by 9" baking pan with foil (see page 14). Put butter in lined pan and place pan in oven to melt butter. Remove pan from oven.

2 Spread coconut and pecans on 15½" by 10½" jelly-roll pan or large cookie sheet; bake, stirring once, until toasted and golden, about 15 minutes. Cool.

3 Meanwhile, place graham crackers between two sheets of plastic wrap or in large zip-tight plastic bag. With rolling pin, crush crackers to make fine crumbs. (Or use food processor with knife blade attached to make crumbs.) Stir crumbs into melted butter in pan. With hands, firmly press crumb mixture onto bottom of pan to form crust.

4 In small bowl, dissolve instant coffee in hot water. Stir in condensed milk.

5 Sprinkle chocolate chips over crust. Top with coconut and pecans. Pour milk mixture evenly over coconut layer.

6 Bake until edges are golden and top browns slightly, about 20 minutes. Cool completely in pan on wire rack.

7 When cool, lift foil, with brownie, out of pan; peel foil away from sides. Cut lengthwise into 6 strips, then cut each strip crosswise into 8 bars. Refrigerate bars until completely set before serving, at least 2 hours.

EACH BAR: ABOUT 145 CALORIES | 2G PROTEIN | 13G CARBOHYDRATE | 10G TOTAL FAT (5G SATURATED) | 1.4G FIBER | 8MG CHOLESTEROL | 40MG SODIUM

MOCHACCINO BROWNIES

Mocha is the combination of coffee and chocolate, and a mochaccino is a cappuccino with chocolate syrup added. Here we adapt the concept to brownies any coffee lover will savor.

ACTIVE TIME: 25 MINUTES · **TOTAL TIME:** 50 MINUTES PLUS COOLING
MAKES: 24 BROWNIES

BROWNIE

1 CUP ALL-PURPOSE FLOUR

¼ TEASPOON SALT

2 TABLESPOONS INSTANT COFFEE OR ESPRESSO-COFFEE POWDER

1 TABLESPOON VERY HOT WATER

½ CUP BUTTER OR MARGARINE (1 STICK)

1 PACKAGE (8 OUNCES) UNSWEETENED CHOCOLATE

2 CUPS GRANULATED SUGAR

4 LARGE EGGS, LIGHTLY BEATEN

1 TEASPOON VANILLA EXTRACT

MOCHACCINO GLAZE

4 TEASPOONS INSTANT COFFEE OR ESPRESSO-COFFEE POWDER

2 TABLESPOONS BUTTER OR MARGARINE, MELTED AND KEPT HOT

2 CUPS CONFECTIONERS' SUGAR

3 TABLESPOONS MILK

1 TEASPOON VANILLA EXTRACT

1   Preheat oven to 350°F. Line 13" by 9" baking pan with foil (see page 14); grease foil.

2   Prepare brownie: In small bowl, with wire whisk, mix flour and salt. In cup, dissolve instant coffee in water; set aside. In 3-quart saucepan, melt butter and chocolate over low heat, stirring frequently, until smooth. Remove from heat; stir in granulated sugar. Add eggs, vanilla, and coffee mixture; stir until blended. Stir flour mixture into chocolate mixture just until blended. Spread batter evenly in prepared pan.

3   Bake until toothpick inserted 2 inches from edge comes out almost clean, 25 to 30 minutes. Cool completely in pan on wire rack.

4   When cool, prepare glaze: In medium bowl, with wire whisk, dissolve coffee in hot melted butter. Stir in confectioners' sugar, milk, and vanilla until smooth.

5   With small metal spatula, spread glaze over cooled brownie. Lift foil, with brownie, out of pan; peel foil away from sides. Cut lengthwise into 4 strips, then cut each strip crosswise into 6 pieces.

EACH BROWNIE: ABOUT 230 CALORIES | 3G PROTEIN | 33G CARBOHYDRATE | 11G TOTAL FAT (9G SATURATED) | 2G FIBER | 49MG CHOLESTEROL | 90MG SODIUM

MEXICAN BROWNIES

These luscious cocoa brownies have a hint of cinnamon and are topped with a creamy coffee-accented frosting.

ACTIVE TIME: 30 MINUTES · TOTAL TIME: 55 MINUTES PLUS COOLING
MAKES: 24 BROWNIES

BROWNIE

- 1 CUP ALL-PURPOSE FLOUR
- 1 CUP UNSWEETENED COCOA
- ½ TEASPOON BAKING POWDER
- ½ TEASPOON GROUND CINNAMON
- ½ TEASPOON SALT
- 1 CUP BUTTER OR MARGARINE (2 STICKS)
- 2 CUPS GRANULATED SUGAR
- 4 LARGE EGGS
- 1 TABLESPOON VANILLA EXTRACT

COFFEE FROSTING

- 1 TABLESPOON INSTANT COFFEE POWDER OR GRANULES
- 2 TABLESPOONS HOT WATER
- 1 TABLESPOON VANILLA EXTRACT
- ¼ CUP PACKED BROWN SUGAR
- 3 TABLESPOONS BUTTER OR MARGARINE
- 1⅓ CUPS CONFECTIONERS' SUGAR

GARNISH

COFFEE BEANS AND/OR CHOPPED SEMISWEET CHOCOLATE

1   Preheat oven to 350°F. Line 13" by 9" baking pan with foil (see page 14); grease foil. In medium bowl, with wire whisk, mix flour, cocoa, baking powder, cinnamon, and salt.

2   In 3-quart saucepan, melt butter over low heat. Remove from heat; stir in granulated sugar. Stir in eggs, one at a time, until well blended; add vanilla. Stir flour mixture into sugar mixture until blended. Spread batter evenly in prepared pan.

3   Bake until toothpick inserted in center of pan comes out almost clean, 25 to 30 minutes. Cool completely in pan on wire rack.

4   When brownie is cool, prepare frosting: In cup, dissolve coffee in water. Stir in vanilla; set aside. In 1-quart saucepan, heat brown sugar and butter over medium heat until mixture melts and bubbles, about 2 minutes. Remove from heat. With wire whisk, stir in coffee mixture; then stir in confectioners' sugar until blended and smooth.

5   With small metal spatula, spread warm frosting over cooled brownie. Let stand 20 minutes to allow frosting to set slightly.

6   When frosting has set, lift foil, with brownie, out of pan; peel foil away from sides. Cut lengthwise into 4 strips, then cut each strip crosswise into 6 pieces. Garnish each brownie with a coffee bean or chopped chocolate.

EACH BROWNIE: ABOUT 225 CALORIES | 2G PROTEIN | 31G CARBOHYDRATE | 11G TOTAL FAT (7G SATURATED) | 1G FIBER | 61MG CHOLESTEROL | 165MG SODIUM

EASY MEXICAN BROWNIES

These thoroughly grownup brownies can be made in time for your coffee break with the help of a box of brownie mix.

ACTIVE TIME: 20 MINUTES · TOTAL TIME: 45 MINUTES PLUS COOLING

MAKES: 24 BROWNIES

---

1 BOX (19½ TO 22½ OUNCES) FAMILY-SIZE 13"X9" BROWNIE MIX

½ TEASPOON GROUND CINNAMON

1 TABLESPOON INSTANT COFFEE POWDER OR GRANULES

2 TABLESPOONS HOT WATER

1 TABLESPOON VANILLA EXTRACT

¼ CUP PACKED BROWN SUGAR

3 TABLESPOONS BUTTER OR MARGARINE

1⅓ CUPS CONFECTIONERS' SUGAR, SIFTED

COFFEE BEANS AND/OR CHOPPED SEMISWEET CHOCOLATE FOR GARNISH

1 Preheat oven to 350°F. Line 13" by 9" baking pan with foil (see page 14); grease foil.

2 Prepare brownie mix according to package directions. Stir in cinnamon. Spread batter evenly in prepared pan.

3 Bake until toothpick inserted in the center of pan comes out almost clean, 25 to 30 minutes. Cool brownie completely in pan on wire rack.

4 In cup, dissolve coffee in water. Stir in vanilla; set aside. In small saucepan, heat brown sugar and butter over medium heat until mixture melts and bubbles, about 2 minutes. Remove from heat. With wire whisk, stir in coffee mixture; then stir in confectioners' sugar until blended and smooth.

5 With small metal spatula, spread warm frosting over cooled brownie. Let stand 20 minutes to allow frosting to set slightly. When frosting has set, lift foil, with brownies, out of pan; peel foil away from sides. Cut lengthwise into 4 strips, then cut each strip crosswise into 6 pieces. Garnish each brownie with a coffee bean or some chopped chocolate.

EACH BROWNIE: ABOUT 196 CALORIES | 2G PROTEIN | 29G CARBOHYDRATE | 9G TOTAL FAT (2G SATURATED) | 1G FIBER | 22MG CHOLESTEROL | 119MG SODIUM

ESPRESSO BROWNIES

A few sneaky tricks make these dreamy mocha bars a low-fat reality. Using cocoa instead of solid chocolate makes a big difference. In addition, corn syrup replaces some of the fat, and egg whites take the place of whole eggs. A little butter in the batter ensures rich flavor.

ACTIVE TIME: 15 MINUTES · TOTAL TIME: 28 MINUTES PLUS COOLING
MAKES: 16 BROWNIES

1 TEASPOON INSTANT ESPRESSO-COFFEE POWDER	3 TABLESPOONS BUTTER OR MARGARINE
1 TEASPOON HOT WATER	¾ CUP SUGAR
¾ CUP ALL-PURPOSE FLOUR	¼ CUP DARK CORN SYRUP
½ CUP UNSWEETENED COCOA	1 TEASPOON VANILLA EXTRACT
½ TEASPOON BAKING POWDER	2 LARGE EGG WHITES
¼ TEASPOON SALT	

1   Preheat oven to 350°F. Line 8" by 8" baking pan with foil (see page 14); grease foil. In cup, dissolve espresso-coffee powder in hot water; set aside.
2   In large bowl, with wire whisk, mix the flour, cocoa, baking powder, and salt.
3   In 2-quart saucepan, melt butter over low heat. Remove from heat. Add sugar, corn syrup, vanilla, egg whites, and espresso mixture and whisk until blended. With heatproof spatula or spoon, stir sugar mixture into flour mixture just until blended. Do not overmix. Pour batter into prepared pan.
4   Bake until toothpick inserted in center comes out almost clean, 18 to 22 minutes. Cool in pan on wire rack at least 1 hour.
5   When cool, lift foil, with brownie, out of pan; peel foil away from sides. Cut into 4 strips, then cut each strip crosswise into 4 pieces. If brownies are difficult to cut, use knife dipped in hot water and dried, repeating as necessary.

EACH BROWNIE: ABOUT 100 CALORIES | 2G PROTEIN | 19G CARBOHYDRATE | 3G TOTAL FAT (2G SATURATED) | 1G FIBER | 6MG CHOLESTEROL | 90MG SODIUM

CAPPUCCINO TRIANGLES

Sweet and sophisticated, these little bites are covered with a coffee-and-cinnamon spiked glaze.

ACTIVE TIME: 45 MINUTES · TOTAL TIME: 1 HOUR 15 MINUTES PLUS COOLING

MAKES: 48 TRIANGLES

COOKIE BAR

- 6   TABLESPOONS BUTTER OR MARGARINE
- 2   TEASPOONS INSTANT ESPRESSO-COFFEE POWDER
- 1¼ CUPS PACKED LIGHT BROWN SUGAR
- 2   TEASPOONS VANILLA EXTRACT
- 2   LARGE EGGS
- 1   CUP ALL-PURPOSE FLOUR
- 2   TEASPOONS BAKING POWDER
- 1   TEASPOON SALT
- ½   TEASPOON GROUND CINNAMON

GLAZE

- 3 TO 4 TEASPOONS MILK OR WATER
- 2   TEASPOONS VANILLA EXTRACT
- 1   TEASPOON INSTANT ESPRESSO-COFFEE POWDER
- 1   CUP CONFECTIONERS' SUGAR
- ¼   TEASPOON GROUND CINNAMON

GARNISH

- 48 ESPRESSO-COFFEE BEANS

1   Preheat oven to 350°F. Line 13" by 9" baking pan with foil (see page 14); grease foil.

2   Prepare cookie bar: In heavy 2-quart saucepan, melt butter with coffee powder over low heat. Remove from heat. With wire whisk, beat in brown sugar, vanilla, and eggs until mixed. With wooden spoon, stir in flour, baking powder, salt, and cinnamon just until blended. Spread batter evenly in prepared pan.

3   Bake until toothpick inserted 2 inches from edge of pan comes out clean, 25 to 30 minutes. Cool completely in pan on wire rack.

4   When cool, lift foil, with cookie bar, out of pan and invert onto wire rack; remove foil. Immediately invert cooking bar again, top side up, onto cutting board.

5   Prepare glaze: In small bowl, with wire whisk or fork, stir the milk, vanilla, and espresso-coffee powder until powder has dissolved. Stir in confectioners' sugar and cinnamon until blended. With small metal spatula, spread glaze evenly over cookie bar.

6   While glaze is still wet, cut cookie bar lengthwise into 4 strips, then cut each strip crosswise into 6 rectangles. Cut each rectangle diagonally in half into triangles. Garnish each triangle with an espresso bean. Let triangles stand until glaze has set, about 30 minutes. Store triangles in tightly covered container, with waxed paper between layers, up to 2 weeks.

EACH TRIANGLE: ABOUT 60 CALORIES | 1G PROTEIN | 10G CARBOHYDRATE | 2G TOTAL FAT (1G SATURATED) | 0G FIBER | 13MG CHOLESTEROL | 85MG SODIUM

BLONDIES, SPICE BARS & SHORTBREAD

Blond Bombshells (page 64)

BLOND BOMBSHELLS

These favorites go from saucepan to baking pan in one easy step.

ACTIVE TIME: 15 MINUTES · TOTAL TIME: 40 MINUTES PLUS COOLING
MAKES: 24 BLONDIES

2½ CUPS ALL-PURPOSE FLOUR

1   TEASPOON BAKING SODA

1   TEASPOON SALT

¾   CUP BUTTER OR MARGARINE
     (1½ STICKS)

1   PACKAGE (1 POUND) DARK OR
     LIGHT BROWN SUGAR

1   TABLESPOON VANILLA EXTRACT

3   LARGE EGGS

3   CUPS MIXED ADD-INS SUCH AS
     COARSELY CHOPPED PECANS OR
     WALNUTS, DRIED CHERRIES OR DRIED
     CRANBERRIES, CHOCOLATE CHIPS,
     TOFFEE CHIPS, AND SWEETENED
     FLAKED COCONUT

1 Preheat oven to 350°F. Line 15½" by 10½" jelly-roll pan with foil (see page 14); grease foil. In medium bowl, with wire whisk, mix flour, baking soda, and salt.

2 In 3- to 4-quart saucepan, melt butter over medium heat. Remove saucepan from heat; stir in sugar and vanilla. Add eggs one at a time; stir until well mixed after each addition. Stir in flour mixture and add-ins just until blended. Spread batter into prepared pan.

3 Bake blondie until toothpick inserted 2 inches from edges comes out almost clean, about 25 minutes. Do not overbake; blondie will firm as it cools. Cool completely in pan on wire rack.

4 When cool, lift foil, with blondie, out of pan; peel foil away from sides. Cut blondie lengthwise into 4 strips, then cut each strip crosswise into 6 pieces.

EACH BLONDIE: ABOUT 265 CALORIES | 3G PROTEIN | 38G CARBOHYDRATE | 12G TOTAL FAT (6G SATURATED) | 2G FIBER | 43MG CHOLESTEROL | 230MG SODIUM

CHOCOLATE SWIRL PEANUT BUTTER BLONDIES

For a different look, you can drop the chocolate and peanut butter doughs in a patchwork on the base then swirl a knife through them for a marbled effect. See page 15 for photo of technique.

ACTIVE TIME: 20 MINUTES · TOTAL TIME: 45 MINUTES PLUS COOLING
MAKES: 24 BLONDIES

2½ CUPS ALL-PURPOSE FLOUR

1½ TEASPOONS BAKING POWDER

½ TEASPOON SALT

3 SQUARES (3 OUNCES) SEMISWEET CHOCOLATE, CHOPPED

1 SQUARE (1 OUNCE) UNSWEETENED CHOCOLATE, CHOPPED

1 CUP CREAMY PEANUT BUTTER

½ CUP BUTTER OR MARGARINE (1 STICK), SOFTENED

1¾ CUPS PACKED LIGHT BROWN SUGAR

3 LARGE EGGS

2 TEASPOONS VANILLA EXTRACT

1 PACKAGE (6 OUNCES) SEMISWEET CHOCOLATE CHIPS (1 CUP)

1 Preheat oven to 350°F. Line 13" by 9" pan with foil (see page 14); do not grease foil. In medium bowl, with wire whisk, mix flour, baking powder, and salt. In heavy 1-quart saucepan, melt semisweet and unsweetened chocolates, stirring frequently, until smooth.

2 In large bowl, with mixer at medium speed, beat peanut butter, butter, and brown sugar until light and fluffy, about 2 minutes. Add eggs one at a time, then vanilla; beat until blended. Reduce speed to low; beat in flour mixture just until blended (dough will be stiff).

3 Place one-third of dough (about 1¾ cups) in separate large bowl. Stir in melted chocolate until blended; stir in ¾ cup chocolate chips.

4 With hand, pat half of remaining plain peanut butter dough onto bottom of prepared pan to form thin layer. In random pattern, drop chocolate dough and remaining plain peanut butter dough on top of peanut butter layer; lightly pat. Sprinkle remaining chocolate chips on top.

5 Bake until toothpick inserted in center comes out clean, 25 to 30 minutes. Cool completely in pan on wire rack.

6 When cool, lift foil, with blondie, out of pan; peel foil away from sides. Cut lengthwise into 4 strips, then cut each strip crosswise into 6 pieces.

EACH BLONDIE: ABOUT 273 CALORIES | 6G PROTEIN | 34G CARBOHYDRATE | 14G TOTAL FAT (6G SATURATED) | 2G FIBER | 37MG CHOLESTEROL | 184MG SODIUM

BUTTERSCOTCH BLONDIES

These rich bars are a pecan lover's dream.

ACTIVE TIME: 15 MINUTES · TOTAL TIME: 35 MINUTES PLUS COOLING
MAKES: 24 BLONDIES

1	CUP ALL-PURPOSE FLOUR	1¾	CUPS PACKED LIGHT BROWN SUGAR
2	TEASPOONS BAKING POWDER	2	TEASPOONS VANILLA EXTRACT
¾	TEASPOON SALT	2	LARGE EGGS, LIGHTLY BEATEN
6	TABLESPOONS BUTTER OR MARGARINE	1	CUP PECANS (4 OUNCES), COARSELY CHOPPED

1 Preheat oven to 350°F. Line 13" by 9" baking pan with foil (see page 14); grease foil.

2 In small bowl, with wire whisk, mix flour, baking powder, and salt. In 3-quart saucepan, melt butter over medium heat. Remove saucepan from heat; stir in brown sugar and vanilla. Add eggs; stir until well mixed. Stir in flour mixture and pecans just until blended. Spread batter evenly in prepared pan.

3 Bake until toothpick inserted 2 inches from edge comes out almost clean, 20 to 25 minutes. Do not overbake; blondie will firm as it cools. Cool completely in pan on wire rack.

4 When cool, lift foil, with blondie, out of pan; peel foil away from sides. Cut lengthwise into 4 strips, then cut each strip crosswise into 6 pieces.

TIP Exposure to air causes brown sugar to dry out, but adding a slice of apple or bread to the box will soften it. Because air can get trapped between its coarse crystals, brown sugar should be firmly packed when measured.

EACH BLONDIE: ABOUT 145 CALORIES | 2G PROTEIN | 20G CARBOHYDRATE | 7G TOTAL FAT (2G SATURATED) | 1G FIBER | 26MG CHOLESTEROL | 150MG SODIUM

LOW-FAT BUTTERSCOTCH BLONDIES

These chewy bars prove that a low-fat dessert can be just as flavorful as its high-fat counterpart. With just three grams of fat per blondie, you can have your "cake" and eat a second one too.

ACTIVE TIME: 15 MINUTES · TOTAL TIME: 50 MINUTES PLUS COOLING
MAKES: 16 BLONDIES

1	CUP ALL-PURPOSE FLOUR	2	LARGE EGG WHITES
½	TEASPOON BAKING POWDER	⅓	CUP DARK CORN SYRUP
¼	TEASPOON SALT	2	TEASPOONS VANILLA EXTRACT
3	TABLESPOONS BUTTER OR MARGARINE	2	TABLESPOONS FINELY CHOPPED PECANS
¾	CUP PACKED DARK BROWN SUGAR		

1   Preheat oven to 350°F. Line 8-inch square baking pan with foil (see page 14); grease foil. In small bowl, with wire whisk, mix flour, baking powder, and salt.

2   In large bowl, with mixer at medium speed, beat butter and brown sugar until well blended, about 2 minutes. Reduce speed to low; beat in egg whites, corn syrup, and vanilla until smooth. Beat in flour mixture just until combined. Spread batter evenly in prepared pan. Sprinkle with finely chopped pecans.

3   Bake until toothpick inserted in center comes out clean and edges are lightly browned, 35 to 40 minutes. Cool completely in pan on wire rack.

4   When cool, lift foil, with blondie, out of pan; peel foil away from sides. Cut into 4 strips, then cut each strip crosswise into 4 pieces.

EACH BLONDIE: ABOUT 117 CALORIES | 1G PROTEIN | 21G CARBOHYDRATE | 3G TOTAL FAT (61G SATURATED) | 0.3G FIBER | 6MG CHOLESTEROL | 94MG SODIUM

SHORTENIN' BREAD

In Scotland, as far back as the twelfth century, shortbread was baked in round pans (sometimes with fluted edges) and cut into wedges.

ACTIVE TIME: 20 MINUTES · **TOTAL TIME:** 45 MINUTES PLUS COOLING
MAKES: 24 WEDGES

¾ CUP BUTTER OR MARGARINE (1½ STICKS), SOFTENED

⅓ CUP PACKED DARK BROWN SUGAR

3 TABLESPOONS GRANULATED SUGAR

1 TEASPOON VANILLA EXTRACT

1¾ CUPS ALL-PURPOSE FLOUR

1 CUP PECANS (4 OUNCES), CHOPPED

1 Preheat oven to 350°F. In large bowl, with mixer at medium-low speed, beat butter, brown and granulated sugars, and vanilla until creamy. Reduce speed to low and beat in flour until blended (dough will be crumbly). With wooden spoon, stir dough until it holds together.

2 Divide dough in half. With hand, pat evenly onto bottoms of two ungreased 8-inch round cake pans. Sprinkle each with pecans; press lightly.

3 Bake until edges are lightly browned and center is firm, 23 to 25 minutes. Transfer pans to wire racks. With small sharp knife, cut each round into 12 wedges. Cool completely in pans on wire racks then use small metal spatula and carefully remove cookies from pan.

EACH WEDGE: ABOUT 130 CALORIES | 1G PROTEIN | 12G CARBOHYDRATE | 9G TOTAL FAT (4G SATURATED) | 1G FIBER | 13MG CHOLESTEROL | 60MG SODIUM

SCOTTISH SHORTBREAD

The combination of cake flour and all-purpose flour makes a tender melt-in-your-mouth shortbread.

ACTIVE TIME: 20 MINUTES · **TOTAL TIME:** 1 HOUR PLUS COOLING
MAKES: 32 WEDGES

1½ CUPS CAKE FLOUR (NOT SELF-RISING)

1½ CUPS ALL-PURPOSE FLOUR

½ CUP SUGAR

¼ TEASPOON SALT

1½ CUPS BUTTER (3 STICKS), CUT INTO PIECES AND SOFTENED, (DO NOT USE MARGARINE)

1 Preheat oven to 325°F. In large bowl, with wire whisk, mix cake and all-purpose flours, sugar, and salt. Knead butter into flour mixture until mixture is well blended and holds together. (Or, in food processor with knife blade attached, pulse cake and all-purpose flours, sugar, and salt to blend. Add butter and pulse until mixture resembles coarse crumbs.)

2 Divide dough in half. With hand, pat evenly onto bottoms of two ungreased 8-inch round cake pans. With fork, prick dough all over to make attractive pattern.

3 Bake until golden, about 40 minutes. Remove from oven; immediately run knife around sides of pans to loosen shortbread, then cut each shortbread round into 16 wedges. Cool completely in pans on wire racks.

4 When cool, with small metal spatula, carefully remove cookies from pans.

EACH WEDGE: ABOUT 128 CALORIES | 1G PROTEIN | 12G CARBOHYDRATE | 9G TOTAL FAT (5G SATURATED) | 1G FIBER | 23MG CHOLESTEROL | 106MG SODIUM

SHORTBREAD BITES

Decked out in red and green sprinkles, these bite-sized treats are almost as fun to make as they are to eat.

ACTIVE TIME: 30 MINUTES · **TOTAL TIME:** 1 HOUR 6 MINUTES PLUS CHILLING AND COOLING
MAKES: 160 BITES

1¼ CUPS ALL-PURPOSE FLOUR

3 TABLESPOONS SUGAR

½ CUP COLD BUTTER (1 STICK), CUT UP (DO NOT USE MARGARINE)

1 TABLESPOON RED AND GREEN NONPAREILS OR SPRINKLES, OR ½ CUP MINI BAKING BITS

1 Preheat oven to 325°F.

2 In food processor with knife blade attached, pulse flour and sugar until combined. Add butter and pulse until dough begins to come together. Place dough in medium bowl. With hand, gently knead in nonpareils or baking bits until evenly blended and dough forms a ball.

3 On lightly floured waxed paper, pat dough into 8" by 5" rectangle; freeze 15 minutes.

4 Cut dough into ½-inch squares. Place squares, ½ inch apart, on ungreased large cookie sheet.

5 Bake until lightly browned on bottom, 18 to 20 minutes. Transfer squares to wire rack to cool. Repeat with remaining dough. Store in tightly covered container at room temperature up to 1 week, or in freezer up to 3 months.

EACH SERVING (4 BITES): ABOUT 40 CALORIES | 0G PROTEIN | 4G CARBOHYDRATE
3G TOTAL FAT (42G SATURATED) | 0G FIBER | 7MG CHOLESTEROL | 25MG SODIUM

GUILT-FREE SPICE BARS

These soft, chewy, guilt-free spice bars—based on hermits, a Colonial New England standby—replace some of the butter or margarine found in traditional baked goods with prune puree, a heart-healthy alternative. They also incorporate soya powder, which is ground finer than soy flour and is more flavorful. It is available in health-food stores.

ACTIVE TIME: 15 MINUTES · TOTAL TIME: 35 MINUTES PLUS COOLING
MAKES: 16 BARS

½   CUP ALL-PURPOSE FLOUR

½   CUP SOYA POWDER (SEE NOTE, ABOVE)

⅓   CUP PACKED DARK BROWN SUGAR

1   TEASPOON GROUND CINNAMON

¾   TEASPOON GROUND GINGER

½   TEASPOON BAKING POWDER

¼   TEASPOON SALT

⅔   CUP PITTED PRUNES, COARSELY CHOPPED

¼   CUP LIGHT (MILD) MOLASSES

2   TABLESPOONS BUTTER OR MARGARINE, SOFTENED

1   LARGE EGG WHITE

1   TEASPOON VANILLA EXTRACT

CONFECTIONERS' SUGAR (OPTIONAL)

1   Preheat oven to 350°F. Line 8-inch square baking pan with foil (see page 14); spray foil evenly with nonstick cooking spray.

2   In medium bowl, with wire whisk, mix flour, soya powder, brown sugar, cinnamon, ginger, baking powder, and salt.

3   In food processor with knife blade attached, puree half the prunes, the molasses, butter, egg white, and vanilla until thick and smooth. Add prune mixture to flour mixture; stir vigorously until well blended (mixture may seem dry at first). Stir in remaining prunes (batter will be very sticky).

4   Spoon batter into prepared pan. Cover with waxed paper. With hand, press on paper until batter is spread in even layer. Discard waxed paper.

5   Bake until edges brown, about 20 minutes. Cool completely in pan on wire rack.

6   When cool, invert onto cutting board and remove foil. Cut square in half, then cut each half crosswise into 8 bars. Store bars, with waxed paper between layers, in tightly covered container up to 2 weeks. Sprinkle with confectioners' sugar just before serving, if you like.

EACH BAR: ABOUT 90 CALORIES | 2G PROTEIN | 17G CARBOHYDRATE | 2G TOTAL FAT (1G SATURATED) | 1G FIBER | 4MG CHOLESTEROL | 71MG SODIUM

FLAPJACKS

In the U.S., the term "flapjacks" refers to pancakes. In England, flapjacks are tasty no-fuss brown sugar and oatmeal wedges. Quick, easy, and delicious—they are a perfect recipe for a young baker.

ACTIVE TIME: 15 MINUTES · TOTAL TIME: 16 MINUTES
MAKES: 16 WEDGES

5 TABLESPOONS BUTTER OR MARGARINE

⅓ CUP PACKED LIGHT BROWN SUGAR

1⅓ CUP OLD-FASHIONED OATS, UNCOOKED

PINCH SALT

1   Preheat oven to 350°F. Line 8-inch round cake pan with foil (see page 14); grease foil.

2   In 2-quart saucepan, melt butter over low heat. Add sugar and cook, stirring, until well blended, 1 minute. Remove from heat; stir in oats and salt until evenly mixed.

3   Sprinkle oat mixture evenly over bottom of prepared pan; with metal spatula, firmly pat down mixture.

4   Bake until golden, 16 to 18 minutes. Let cool in pan on wire rack 10 minutes.

5   Lift foil, with round, out of pan; peel foil away from sides. While still warm, cut round into 16 wedges. Transfer foil with flapjacks to wire rack to cool completely.

EACH WEDGE: ABOUT 100 CALORIES | 2G PROTEIN | 13G CARBOHYDRATE | 5G TOTAL FAT (3G SATURATED) | 1G FIBER | 10MG CHOLESTEROL | 50MG SODIUM

GLAZED GINGER BARS

These are perfect holiday sweets for an old-fashioned swap with friends.

ACTIVE TIME: 25 MINUTES · TOTAL TIME: 50 MINUTES PLUS COOLING
MAKES: 32 BARS

GINGER BARS

2 CUPS ALL-PURPOSE FLOUR

½ TEASPOON GROUND GINGER

½ TEASPOON GROUND CINNAMON

½ TEASPOON BAKING SODA

⅛ TEASPOON SALT

½ CUP RAISINS

¾ CUP BUTTER OR MARGARINE (1½ STICKS), SOFTENED

¾ CUP PACKED DARK BROWN SUGAR

½ CUP DARK MOLASSES

1 LARGE EGG

2 TABLESPOONS GRATED, PEELED FRESH GINGER

ORANGE GLAZE

1 ORANGE

1½ CUPS CONFECTIONERS' SUGAR, SIFTED

2 TABLESPOONS BUTTER OR MARGARINE, MELTED

1 TEASPOON VANILLA EXTRACT

⅛ TEASPOON SALT

1   Preheat oven to 350°F. Line 13" by 9" baking pan with foil (see page 14); grease foil.

2   Prepare bars: In medium bowl, with wire whisk, mix flour, ground ginger, cinnamon, baking soda, and salt. Add raisins; toss to combine.

3   In large bowl, with mixer at medium speed, beat butter, brown sugar, and molasses until light and fluffy, about 2 minutes. Beat in egg and fresh ginger until well combined. Reduce speed to low and beat in flour mixture just until blended. Spread batter evenly in prepared pan.

4   Bake until toothpick inserted in center comes out clean, about 25 minutes. Transfer pan to wire rack.

5   Meanwhile, prepare glaze: From orange, grate ½ teaspoon peel and squeeze 2 tablespoons juice. In medium bowl, with wire whisk, mix orange peel and juice, confectioners' sugar, butter, vanilla, and salt until smooth. Spread glaze over hot pastry. Cool in pan on wire rack.

6   When cool, lift foil, with pastry, out of pan; peel foil away from sides. Cut lengthwise into 8 strips, then cut each strip crosswise into 4 bars.

EACH BAR: ABOUT 140 CALORIES | 1G PROTEIN | 22G CARBOHYDRATE | 6G TOTAL FAT (3G SATURATED) | 0G FIBER | 21MG CHOLESTEROL | 100MG SODIUM

LINZER BARS

These pretty jam-filled bars are easier than they look. A layer of dough is topped with a layer of jam, then the rest of the dough is piped onto the top of the bars to create a sweet lattice effect.

ACTIVE TIME: 45 MINUTES · TOTAL TIME: 1 HOUR 15 MINUTES PLUS COOLING
MAKES: 32 BARS

1¾ CUPS ALL-PURPOSE FLOUR

1 TEASPOON GROUND CINNAMON

½ TEASPOON BAKING POWDER

¼ TEASPOON SALT

1 CUP HAZELNUTS (4 OUNCES), TOASTED (PAGE 31)

½ CUP GRANULATED SUGAR

¾ CUP BUTTER OR MARGARINE (1½ STICKS), SOFTENED

¼ CUP PACKED LIGHT BROWN SUGAR

1 LARGE EGG

1 JAR (12 OUNCES) RASPBERRY JAM CONFECTIONERS' SUGAR (OPTIONAL)

1 Preheat oven to 350°F. Line 13" by 9" baking pan with foil (see page 14). In medium bowl, with wire whisk, mix flour, cinnamon, baking powder, and salt. In food processor with knife blade attached, process hazelnuts and granulated sugar to a coarse powder.

2 In large bowl, with mixer at medium speed, beat butter and brown sugar until creamy. Add egg and hazelnut mixture and beat until well blended. Reduce speed to low; gradually beat in flour mixture just until blended.

3 Reserve 1½ cups dough for top layer. With floured fingers, press remaining dough firmly onto bottom of prepared pan. Spread jam evenly over dough, leaving ¼-inch border all around.

4 Place reserved dough in sturdy pastry bag fitted with ¼-inch round tip. (Dough is too stiff to use plastic bag for piping; it may burst.) Pipe dough in diagonal lines, ¾ inch apart, over jam. Pipe around inside of pan to create finished edge.

5 Bake until dough is lightly browned, 30 to 35 minutes. Cool completely in pan on wire rack.

6 When cool, lift foil, with bar, out of pan; peel foil away from sides. Cut lengthwise into 4 strips, then cut each strip crosswise into 8 bars. Store in tightly covered container, with waxed paper between layers, at room temperature up to 3 days, or in freezer up to 1 month. Sprinkle with confectioners' sugar to serve, if you like.

EACH BAR: ABOUT 140 CALORIES | 2G PROTEIN | 18G CARBOHYDRATE | 7G TOTAL FAT
(3G SATURATED) | 1G FIBER | 19MG CHOLESTEROL | 75MG SODIUM

ITALIAN TRICOLORS

These pretty bars, featuring the colors of the Italian flag, are often found in Italian bakeries. Now you can whip up a batch at home.

ACTIVE TIME: 1 HOUR · TOTAL TIME: 1 HOUR 10 MINUTES PLUS COOLING AND CHILLING
MAKES: 36 BARS

- 1 TUBE OR CAN (7 TO 8 OUNCES) ALMOND PASTE, BROKEN INTO SMALL PIECES
- ¾ CUP BUTTER OR MARGARINE (1½ STICKS), SOFTENED
- ¾ CUP SUGAR
- ½ TEASPOON ALMOND EXTRACT
- 3 LARGE EGGS
- 1 CUP ALL-PURPOSE FLOUR
- ¼ TEASPOON SALT
- 15 DROPS RED FOOD COLORING
- 15 DROPS GREEN FOOD COLORING
- ⅔ CUP APRICOT PRESERVES
- 3 SQUARES (3 OUNCES) SEMISWEET CHOCOLATE
- 1 TEASPOON VEGETABLE SHORTENING

1 Preheat oven to 350°F. Grease three 8-inch square disposable or metal baking pans. Line bottoms of pans with waxed paper; grease and flour waxed paper.

2 In large bowl, with mixer at medium-high speed, beat almond paste, butter, sugar, and almond extract until well blended (there will be some small lumps of almond paste remaining). Reduce speed to medium; beat in eggs, one at a time, until blended. Reduce speed to low; beat in flour and salt just until combined.

3 Transfer one-third of batter (about 1 rounded cup) to small bowl. Transfer half of remaining batter to another small bowl. (You should have equal amounts of batter in each bowl.) Stir red food coloring into one portion of batter until evenly blended. Repeat with green food coloring and another portion of batter, leaving third portion untinted. (Batters may still have small lumps of almond paste remaining.)

4 Spoon untinted batter into one prepared pan. With metal spatula (offset, if possible), spread batter evenly (layer will be about ¼ inch thick). Repeat with red batter in second pan. Repeat with green batter in remaining pan.

5   Bake until layers are set and toothpick inserted in center of layers comes out clean, 10 to 12 minutes, rotating pans between upper and lower oven racks halfway through baking.

6   Cool in pans on wire racks 5 minutes. Run thin knife around sides of pans to loosen layers. Invert layers onto racks, leaving waxed paper in place; cool completely.

7   When layers are cool, press apricot preserves through coarse sieve into small bowl to remove any large pieces of fruit. Remove waxed paper from green layer. Invert green layer onto flat plate or small cutting board; spread with half of apricot preserves. Remove waxed paper from untinted layer; invert onto green layer. Spread with remaining apricot preserves. Remove waxed paper from red layer; invert onto untinted layer.

8   In 1-quart saucepan, heat chocolate and shortening over low heat, stirring frequently, until melted. Spread melted chocolate mixture on top of red layer (not on sides); refrigerate until chocolate is firm, at least 1 hour. If you like, after chocolate has set, cover and refrigerate stacked layers up to 3 days before cutting and serving.

9   To serve, with serrated knife, trim edges (about ¼ inch from each side). Cut stacked layers into 6 strips. Cut each strip crosswise into 6 pieces.

EACH BAR: ABOUT 125 CALORIES | 2G PROTEIN | 15G CARBOHYDRATE | 7G TOTAL FAT (3G SATURATED) | 1G FIBER | 29MG CHOLESTEROL | 65MG SODIUM

FRUITY SNACK & DESSERT BARS

Date Bars (page 80)

DATE BARS

A luscious brown-sugar streusel tops off moist date bars. To chop the dates, use scissors and dip the blades in water when they get sticky.

ACTIVE TIME: 40 MINUTES · **TOTAL TIME:** 1 HOUR 25 MINUTES PLUS COOLING
MAKES: 12 BARS

OAT CRUST AND TOPPING

1¼ CUPS ALL-PURPOSE FLOUR

1   CUP OLD-FASHIONED OR QUICK-COOKING OATS, UNCOOKED

½   CUP PACKED LIGHT BROWN SUGAR

½   CUP BUTTER (1 STICK), SOFTENED

¼   TEASPOON BAKING SODA

¼   TEASPOON GROUND CINNAMON

¼   TEASPOON SALT

DATE FILLING

1   CONTAINER (10 OUNCES) PITTED DATES, CHOPPED

¾   CUP WATER

2   TABLESPOONS PACKED LIGHT BROWN SUGAR

1   Preheat oven to 375°F. Line 9-inch square baking pan with foil (see page 14); grease foil.

2   Prepare crust and topping: In large bowl, with hand, mix flour, oats, brown sugar, butter, baking soda, cinnamon, and salt until mixture comes together. Transfer 2 cups mixture to prepared pan; reserve remaining mixture for topping. With hand, press mixture onto bottom of prepared pan. Bake 10 minutes. Turn off oven. Cool crust completely in pan on wire rack.

3   While crust is cooling, prepare filling: In 2-quart saucepan, cook dates, water, and brown sugar over medium heat, stirring frequently, until mixture thickens and all liquid has been absorbed, 6 to 8 minutes. Spoon date filling into bowl; cover and refrigerate until cool, about 30 minutes.

4   When filling is cool, preheat oven to 375°F. Spread filling over cooled crust; sprinkle evenly with reserved crumb mixture.

5   Bake until topping is golden, 35 to 40 minutes. Cool completely in pan on wire rack.

6   When cool, lift foil, with pastry, out of pan; peel foil away from sides. Cut into 4 strips, then cut each strip crosswise into 3 pieces.

EACH BAR: ABOUT 275 CALORIES | 4G PROTEIN | 47G CARBOHYDRATE | 9G TOTAL FAT (5G SATURATED) | 3G FIBER | 21MG CHOLESTEROL | 155MG SODIUM

WHOLE-WHEAT FIG BARS

These nutrition-packed low-fat bars make a yummy breakfast for children or adults.

ACTIVE TIME: 15 MINUTES · **TOTAL TIME:** 35 MINUTES PLUS COOLING

MAKES: 12 BARS

- 4 OUNCES DRIED CALIMYRNA FIGS (ABOUT ¾ CUP)
- ½ CUP ALL-PURPOSE FLOUR
- ½ CUP WHOLE-WHEAT FLOUR
- ⅓ CUP PACKED DARK BROWN SUGAR
- 1 TEASPOON GROUND CINNAMON
- ½ TEASPOON GROUND GINGER

- ½ TEASPOON BAKING POWDER
- ¼ TEASPOON SALT
- ⅓ CUP LIGHT (MILD) MOLASSES
- 2 TABLESPOONS BUTTER OR MARGARINE, MELTED
- 1 TEASPOON VANILLA
- 1 LARGE EGG WHITE

1 Preheat oven to 350°F. Line 8-inch square baking pan with foil (see page 14); grease foil.

2 With kitchen shears, cut stems from figs; cut figs into small pieces.

3 In large bowl, with spoon, stir figs, all-purpose flour, whole-wheat flour, brown sugar, cinnamon, ginger, baking powder, and salt until mixed. Stir in molasses, butter, vanilla, and egg white just until blended and evenly moistened. With metal spatula, spread batter evenly in prepared pan (batter will be sticky).

4 Bake until toothpick inserted in center comes out clean, 20 to 25 minutes. Cool completely in pan on wire rack.

5 When cool, lift foil, with pastry, out of pan; peel foil away from sides. Cut into 3 strips, then cut each strip crosswise into 4 pieces.

EACH BAR: ABOUT 130 CALORIES | 2G PROTEIN | 26G CARBOHYDRATE | 2G TOTAL FAT (1G SATURATED) | 2G FIBER | 5MG CHOLESTEROL | 84MG SODIUM

LEMON CRUMBLE BARS

To reduce the prep time of these luscious almond-topped bars, we used store-bought lemon curd for the filling and made the dough and topping in the food processor.

ACTIVE TIME: 25 MINUTES · **TOTAL TIME:** 1 HOUR PLUS COOLING

MAKES: 24 BARS

1¼ CUPS ALL-PURPOSE FLOUR

½ CUP PACKED LIGHT BROWN SUGAR

¼ TEASPOON BAKING SODA

½ CUP COLD BUTTER OR MARGARINE (1 STICK), CUT INTO PIECES

¼ CUP WHOLE NATURAL ALMONDS (WITH SKINS), COARSELY CHOPPED

½ CUP JARRED LEMON CURD

½ TEASPOON FRESHLY GRATED LEMON PEEL

1 Preheat oven to 350°F. Line 9-inch square baking pan with foil (see page 14). In food processor, with knife blade attached, process flour, sugar, and baking soda until mixed. Add butter and pulse just until mixture resembles coarse crumbs. Transfer ½ cup crumb mixture to small bowl and stir in almonds; reserve. Press remaining mixture firmly onto bottom of prepared pan.

2 In another small bowl, mix lemon curd and lemon peel; spread mixture over dough, leaving a ¼-inch border all around. Crumble reserved dough over curd.

3 Bake until topping is browned, 35 to 40 minutes. Cool completely in pan on wire rack.

4 When cool, lift foil, with pastry, out of pan; peel foil away from sides. Cut into 8 strips, then cut each strip crosswise into 3 bars.

EACH BAR: ABOUT 105 CALORIES | 1G PROTEIN | 15G CARBOHYDRATE | 5G TOTAL FAT (3G SATURATED) | 0.5G FIBER | 11MG CHOLESTEROL | 60MG SODIUM

JAM CRUMBLE BARS

A food processor makes quick work of these delicious bars. For variety, spread alternating stripes of different colored jams over the crust or drop spoonfuls of contrasting jams and swirl them together for a marbled effect. See page 15 for photo of technique.

ACTIVE TIME: 15 MINUTES · **TOTAL TIME:** 1 HOUR PLUS COOLING

MAKES: 16 BARS

1¼ CUPS ALL-PURPOSE FLOUR

½ CUP PACKED LIGHT BROWN SUGAR

¼ TEASPOON BAKING SODA

¼ TEASPOON GROUND CINNAMON

½ CUP COLD BUTTER OR MARGARINE (1 STICK), CUT INTO PIECES

¼ CUP PECANS, CHOPPED

½ CUP JAM (SUCH AS RASPBERRY OR BLACKBERRY)

1 Preheat oven to 350°F. Line 9-inch square baking pan with foil (see page 14). In food processor with knife blade attached, process flour, brown sugar, baking soda, and cinnamon until mixed. Add butter and process until mixture resembles coarse crumbs and, when pressed, holds together. Transfer ½ cup crumb mixture to small bowl; stir in pecans. Reserve for topping. Press remaining mixture firmly onto bottom of prepared pan.

2 With small metal spatula, spread jam evenly over dough, leaving ½-inch border all around. With fingers, crumble reserved crumb mixture over jam.

3 Bake until top and edges are browned, 40 to 45 minutes. Cool completely in pan on wire rack.

4 When cool, lift foil, with pastry, out of pan; peel foil away from sides. Cut pastry into 4 strips; then cut each strip crosswise into 4 pieces.

EACH BAR: ABOUT 150 CALORIES | 1G PROTEIN | 21G CARBOHYDRATE | 7G TOTAL FAT (4G SATURATED) | 0.5G FIBER | 16MG CHOLESTEROL | 85MG SODIUM

BLUEBERRY CRUMB BARS

These tasty bars will literally disappear from the platter. Why not make a double batch?

ACTIVE TIME: 30 MINUTES · **TOTAL TIME:** 1 HOUR 25 MINUTES PLUS COOLING
MAKES: 36 BARS

SHORTBREAD CRUST

1   CUP BUTTER OR MARGARINE (2 STICKS), SOFTENED

⅔ CUP CONFECTIONERS' SUGAR

1   TEASPOON VANILLA EXTRACT

2½ CUPS ALL-PURPOSE FLOUR

BLUEBERRY FILLING

3   PINTS BLUEBERRIES

½ CUP GRANULATED SUGAR

3   TABLESPOONS CORNSTARCH

2   TABLESPOONS WATER

STREUSEL TOPPING

⅔ CUP OLD-FASHIONED OR QUICK-COOKING OATS, UNCOOKED

½ CUP ALL-PURPOSE FLOUR

⅓ CUP PACKED BROWN SUGAR

¼ TEASPOON GROUND CINNAMON

½ CUP BUTTER OR MARGARINE (1 STICK)

1 Prepare crust: Preheat oven to 375°F. Line 15½" by 10½" jelly-roll pan with foil (see page 14). In large bowl, with mixer at medium speed, beat butter, confectioners' sugar, and vanilla until light and fluffy. Reduce speed to low; beat in flour just until combined. With hand, press dough firmly onto bottom of prepared pan. Bake until crust is golden brown, 20 minutes. Cool slightly in pan on wire rack.

2 Meanwhile, prepare filling: In 3-quart saucepan, combine blueberries, granulated sugar, cornstarch, and water; heat to boiling over medium-high heat, stirring frequently. Boil 1 minute; remove from heat.

3 Prepare topping: In medium bowl, stir oats, flour, brown sugar, and cinnamon. With pastry blender or two knives used scissor-fashion, cut in butter until mixture resembles coarse crumbs.

4 Spread blueberry mixture evenly over cooled crust. Sprinkle topping over blueberries. Bake until blueberry mixture bubbles and top is lightly browned, 35 to 40 minutes. Cool completely in pan on wire rack.

5 When cool, lift foil, with pastry, out of pan; peel foil away from sides. Cut lengthwise into 6 strips, then cut each strip crosswise into 6 bars.

EACH BAR: ABOUT 165 CALORIES | 2G PROTEIN | 21G CARBOHYDRATE | 79G TOTAL FAT (5G SATURATED) | 1G FIBER | 22MG CHOLESTEROL | 85MG SODIUM

RAISIN-SPICE BARS

You don't need a mixer to make these toothsome cookies, which are reminiscent of the New England favorite, hermits (see page 95).

ACTIVE TIME: 10 MINUTES · **TOTAL TIME:** 28 MINUTES PLUS COOLING

MAKES: 24 BARS

2 CUPS ALL-PURPOSE FLOUR	2 LARGE EGGS
⅔ CUP PACKED LIGHT BROWN SUGAR	⅔ CUP LIGHT (MILD) MOLASSES
2 TEASPOONS GROUND CINNAMON	6 TABLESPOONS BUTTER OR MARGARINE, MELTED
1½ TEASPOONS GROUND GINGER	
½ TEASPOON BAKING SODA	2 TEASPOONS VANILLA EXTRACT
½ TEASPOON SALT	¾ CUP DARK SEEDLESS RAISINS

1 Preheat oven to 375°F. Line 13" by 9" baking pan with foil (see page 14); grease foil.

2 In large bowl, with wooden spoon, stir flour, brown sugar, cinnamon, ginger, baking soda, and salt until combined. Stir in eggs, molasses, butter, and vanilla just until blended. Stir in raisins. Spread batter evenly in prepared pan.

3 Bake until golden around edges, 18 to 22 minutes. Cool completely in pan on wire rack.

4 When cool, lift foil, with pastry, out of pan; peel foil away from sides. Cut lengthwise into 6 strips, then cut each strip crosswise into 4 pieces.

EACH BAR: ABOUT 135 CALORIES | 2G PROTEIN | 24G CARBOHYDRATE | 4G TOTAL FAT (2G SATURATED) | 1G FIBER | 25MG CHOLESTEROL | 115MG SODIUM

APPLE CRUMB SQUARES

These three-layer bars deliver all the flavor of an apple pie packed into tidy, bite-size portions.

ACTIVE TIME: 45 MINUTES · **TOTAL TIME:** 1 HOUR 45 MINUTES PLUS COOLING
MAKES: 24 BARS

CRUMB TOPPING

1   CUP ALL-PURPOSE FLOUR

1   CUP PECANS OR WALNUTS, COARSELY CHOPPED

½   CUP BUTTER OR MARGARINE (1 STICK), SLIGHTLY SOFTENED

½   CUP PACKED LIGHT OR DARK BROWN SUGAR

1   TABLESPOON VANILLA EXTRACT

1   TEASPOON GROUND CINNAMON

CRUST

3   CUPS ALL-PURPOSE FLOUR

⅓   CUP GRANULATED SUGAR

¼   TEASPOON SALT

¾   CUP COLD BUTTER OR MARGARINE (1½ STICKS)

APPLE FILLING

4   POUNDS GREEN COOKING APPLES SUCH AS GRANNY SMITH, PEELED, CORED, AND CUT INTO ½-INCH CHUNKS

4   TABLESPOONS BUTTER OR MARGARINE

¾   CUP DARK SEEDLESS RAISINS OR DRIED CURRANTS

½   CUP LIGHT OR DARK BROWN SUGAR, PACKED

¾   TEASPOON GROUND CINNAMON

1   TABLESPOON CORNSTARCH

3   TABLESPOONS FRESH LEMON JUICE

1   Prepare crumb topping: In medium bowl, with fingertips, mix all topping ingredients until mixture comes together. Shape into a ball; wrap in plastic wrap and refrigerate to use later.

2   Preheat oven to 375°F. Line 15½" by 10½" jelly-roll pan with foil (see page 14); lightly grease foil.

3   Prepare crust: In large bowl, with fork, mix flour, granulated sugar, and salt. With pastry cutter or two knives used scissor-fashion, blend butter in until mixture resembles fine crumbs. With hand, press evenly into bottom of prepared pan. Bake 20 to 24 minutes or until golden brown (crust may crack slightly).

4   Meanwhile, prepare apple filling: In nonstick 12-inch skillet, cook apples, butter, raisins, brown sugar, and cinnamon over medium heat 25 to 30 minutes or until apples are very tender and most liquid has evaporated, stirring occasionally. In cup, mix cornstarch and lemon juice. Stir lemon-juice mixture into apple mixture and cook, stirring, until filling thickens.

5 Spread filling over hot crust. Break topping into chunks and scatter over all. Bake 40 minutes or until topping browns. Cool completely in pan on wire rack.

6 To serve, lift foil, with pastry, out of pan; peel foil away from sides. Cut lengthwise into 4 strips, then cut each strip crosswise into 6 squares.

EACH BAR: ABOUT 315 CALORIES | 3G PROTEIN | 42G CARBOHYDRATE | 16G TOTAL FAT (8G SATURATED) | 3G FIBER | 33MG CHOLESTEROL | 155MG SODIUM

DATE-AND-NUT SQUARES

A chewy, wholesome bar that is extremely easy to make and requires very little cleanup.

ACTIVE TIME: 15 MINUTES · **TOTAL TIME:** 45 MINUTES PLUS COOLING
MAKES: 16 SQUARES

½ CUP BUTTER OR MARGARINE (1 STICK)

1 CUP PACKED LIGHT BROWN SUGAR

1¼ CUPS ALL-PURPOSE FLOUR

1 TEASPOON BAKING SODA

1 CUP PECANS (4 OUNCES), CHOPPED

1 CUP PITTED DATES, CHOPPED

1 LARGE EGG

1 Preheat oven to 350°F. Line 9-inch square baking pan with foil (see page 14); grease foil.

2 In 3-quart saucepan, melt butter and brown sugar over medium-low heat, stirring occasionally, until smooth. Remove from heat. With wooden spoon, beat in flour, baking soda, pecans, dates, and egg until well blended. Spread batter evenly in prepared pan.

3 Bake until toothpick inserted in center comes out clean, 30 to 35 minutes. Cool completely in pan on wire rack.

4 When cool, lift foil, with pastry, out of pan; peel foil away from sides. Cut into 4 strips, then cut each strip crosswise into 4 squares.

EACH SQUARE: ABOUT 221 CALORIES | 2G PROTEIN | 30G CARBOHYDRATE | 11G TOTAL FAT (4G SATURATED) | 2G FIBER | 29MG CHOLESTEROL | 147MG SODIUM

APRICOT CRUMB BARS

Cool the filling and the crust before assembling the layers to keep the crust from crumbling when you spread the filling over it.

ACTIVE TIME: 35 MINUTES · **TOTAL TIME:** 1 HOUR 15 MINUTES PLUS COOLING
MAKES: 40 BARS

APRICOT FILLING

1½ CUPS DRIED APRICOTS (12 OUNCES)

1½ CUPS WATER

¼ CUP GRANULATED SUGAR

SHORTBREAD CRUST

¾ CUP BUTTER OR MARGARINE
    (1½ STICKS), SOFTENED

½ CUP CONFECTIONERS' SUGAR

½ TEASPOON VANILLA EXTRACT

2 CUPS ALL-PURPOSE FLOUR

STREUSEL TOPPING

½ CUP OLD-FASHIONED OR QUICK-
    COOKING OATS, UNCOOKED

½ CUP PACKED LIGHT BROWN SUGAR

⅓ CUP ALL-PURPOSE FLOUR

2 TABLESPOONS BUTTER OR
    MARGARINE

1 Prepare filling: In 1-quart saucepan, combine apricots and water; heat to boiling over medium heat. Reduce heat and simmer, covered, until tender (some water will remain), about 25 minutes. With wooden spoon or potato masher, mash until smooth. Stir in granulated sugar; cool to room temperature.

2 Prepare crust: Preheat oven to 375°F. Line 13" by 9" baking pan with foil (see page 14); lightly grease foil. In large bowl, with mixer at medium speed, beat butter and confectioners' sugar until light and fluffy. Beat in vanilla. Stir in flour until well combined. With hand, pat dough firmly onto bottom of prepared pan. Bake until golden brown and set, about 15 minutes. Cool to room temperature in pan on wire rack.

3 Prepare topping: In medium bowl, stir together oats, brown sugar, and flour. With fingertips, mix in butter until mixture resembles coarse crumbs. Spread cooled filling over crust. Scatter topping over filling.

4 Bake until lightly browned, about 25 minutes. Cool completely in pan on wire rack.

5 When cool, lift foil, with pastry, out of pan; peel foil away from sides. Cut lengthwise into 5 strips, then cut each strip crosswise into 8 pieces.

EACH BAR: ABOUT 110 CALORIES | 1G PROTEIN | 17G CARBOHYDRATE | 5G TOTAL FAT (3G SATURATED) | 1G FIBER | 12MG CHOLESTEROL | 50MG SODIUM

LEBKUCHEN

In addition to possessing great texture, these chewy spice bars are loaded with flavor. Plus, they keep so well they are the perfect make-ahead treats.

ACTIVE TIME: 15 MINUTES · **TOTAL TIME:** 45 MINUTES PLUS COOLING
MAKES: 64 BARS

1 BOX (16 OUNCES) DARK BROWN SUGAR (2¼ CUPS PACKED)

4 LARGE EGGS

1½ CUPS ALL-PURPOSE FLOUR

1½ TEASPOONS GROUND CINNAMON

1 TEASPOON BAKING POWDER

¾ TEASPOON GROUND CLOVES

1 CUP WALNUTS, COARSELY CHOPPED

1 CUP DARK SEEDLESS RAISINS OR ¾ CUP DICED MIXED CANDIED FRUIT

½ CUP CONFECTIONERS' SUGAR

1 TABLESPOON FRESH LEMON JUICE

1 Preheat oven to 350°F. Line 13" by 9" baking pan with foil (see page 14); grease foil.

2 In large bowl, with mixer at medium speed, beat brown sugar and eggs until well mixed, about 1 minute, occasionally scraping bowl with rubber spatula. Reduce speed to low; gradually beat in flour, cinnamon, baking powder, and cloves until blended, occasionally scraping bowl. Stir in walnuts and raisins.

3 Spoon mixture into pan and spread evenly. Bake 30 minutes. Cool completely in pan on wire rack.

4 In medium bowl, mix confectioners' sugar and lemon juice. Drizzle sugar icing over Lebkuchen. Let stand 10 minutes to allow icing to set. Transfer foil to cutting board. Cut lengthwise into 8 strips, then cut each strip crosswise into 8 bars. Store bars in tightly covered container, with waxed paper between layers, at room temperature up to 2 weeks, or in freezer up to 3 months.

EACH BAR: ABOUT 65 CALORIES | 1G PROTEIN | 12G CARBOHYDRATE | 2G TOTAL FAT (2G SATURATED) | 0G FIBER | 13MG CHOLESTEROL | 15MG SODIUM

BREAKFAST GRANOLA BARS

Moist, delicious, and lower in fat than many store-bought snack bars, these are sure to be a winner with everyone in the family.

ACTIVE TIME: 15 MINUTES · **TOTAL TIME:** 45 MINUTES PLUS COOLING
MAKES: 24 BARS

---

2 CUPS OLD-FASHIONED OATS, UNCOOKED	¾ TEASPOON SALT
1 CUP ALL-PURPOSE FLOUR	¾ TEASPOON GROUND CINNAMON
¾ CUP PACKED LIGHT BROWN SUGAR	½ CUP VEGETABLE OIL
¾ CUP DARK SEEDLESS RAISINS	½ CUP HONEY
½ CUP TOASTED WHEAT GERM	1 LARGE EGG
	2 TEASPOONS VANILLA EXTRACT

1 Preheat oven to 350°F. Line 13" by 9" baking pan with foil (see page 14); grease foil.

2 In large bowl, with wooden spoon, mix oats, flour, brown sugar, raisins, wheat germ, salt, and cinnamon until combined. Add oil, honey, egg, and vanilla; stir until blended. With wet hand, pat oat mixture into prepared pan.

3 Bake until pale golden around the edges, 30 to 35 minutes. Cool completely in pan on wire rack.

4 When cool, lift foil, with pastry, from pan; peel foil away from sides. Cut lengthwise into 4 strips, then cut each strip crosswise into 6 pieces.

EACH BAR: ABOUT 185 CALORIES | 4G PROTEIN | 30G CARBOHYDRATE | 6G TOTAL FAT (1G SATURATED) | 1.4G FIBER | 9MG CHOLESTEROL | 75MG SODIUM

GRANOLA SNACK BARS

Bake a pan of these snacks and you'll never go back to the boxed stuff. They're super-easy and fun to make with kids—and far more economical than store-bought granola bars.

ACTIVE TIME: 20 MINUTES · **TOTAL TIME:** 50 MINUTES

MAKES: 18 BARS

- 2 CUPS OLD-FASHIONED OATS, UNCOOKED
- ¾ CUP TOASTED WHEAT GERM
- ¾ CUP CHOPPED WALNUTS
- ¾ CUP DRIED CRANBERRIES
- 2 TABLESPOONS PACKED LIGHT BROWN SUGAR

- 2 TEASPOONS GROUND CINNAMON
- ½ TEASPOON SALT
- ½ CUP HONEY
- ½ CUP VEGETABLE OIL
- 2 LARGE EGG WHITES

1 Preheat oven to 325°F. Line 13" by 9" pan with foil (see page 14); spray foil with cooking spray.

2 In glass pie plate, spread oats; microwave on High, in 1-minute increments, 4 to 5 minutes or until fragrant and golden, stirring occasionally. Cool to room temperature.

3 In large bowl, combine oats, wheat germ, walnuts, cranberries, brown sugar, cinnamon, and salt. Stir in honey, oil, and egg whites until well mixed. Transfer to prepared pan. Using wet hand, press into even layer.

4 Bake 32 to 35 minutes or until dark golden. Cool completely in pan on wire rack.

5 When cool, lift foil, with pastry, out of pan; peel foil away from sides. Cut lengthwise into 6 strips, then cut each strip crosswise into thirds. (You should have roughly 4¼" by 1½" bars.) Store in tightly sealed container at room temperature up to 1 week, or in freezer up to 1 month.

EACH BAR: ABOUT 190 CALORIES | 4G PROTEIN | 23G CARBOHYDRATE | 10G TOTAL FAT (1G SATURATED) | 2G FIBER | 0MG CHOLESTEROL | 70MG SODIUM

HERMIT BARS

Originating in New England in clipper-ship days, these spicy fruit bars got their name because they keep so long. Sailors would stow them away "like hermits" for snacking on extended voyages.

ACTIVE TIME: 20 MINUTES · **TOTAL TIME:** 35 MINUTES PLUS COOLING
MAKES: 32 BARS

2	CUPS ALL-PURPOSE FLOUR	1	CUP PACKED BROWN SUGAR
1	TEASPOON GROUND CINNAMON	½	CUP BUTTER OR MARGARINE (1 STICK), SOFTENED
½	TEASPOON BAKING POWDER	⅓	CUP DARK MOLASSES
½	TEASPOON BAKING SODA	1	LARGE EGG
½	TEASPOON GROUND GINGER	1	CUP DARK SEEDLESS RAISINS
¼	TEASPOON GROUND NUTMEG	1	CUP PECANS (4 OUNCES), TOASTED (SEE PAGE 31) AND COARSELY CHOPPED (OPTIONAL)
¼	TEASPOON SALT		
⅛	TEASPOON GROUND CLOVES		

1 Preheat oven to 350°F. Grease and flour two large cookie sheets.

2 In large bowl, with wire whisk, mix flour, cinnamon, baking powder, baking soda, ginger, nutmeg, salt, and cloves.

3 In separate large bowl, with mixer at medium speed, beat brown sugar and butter until light and fluffy. Beat in molasses until well combined. Beat in egg. With mixer at low speed, beat in flour mixture just until blended, occasionally scraping bowl with rubber spatula. With spoon, stir in raisins and pecans, if using, just until combined.

4 Divide dough into quarters. With lightly floured hands, shape each quarter into 12" by 1½" log. On each prepared cookie sheet, place 2 logs, leaving about 3 inches in between.

5 Bake until logs flatten and edges are firm, 13 to 15 minutes, rotating cookie sheets between upper and lower oven racks halfway through baking. Cool logs on cookie sheets on wire racks 15 minutes.

6 Transfer logs to cutting board. Slice each log crosswise into 8 bars. Transfer to wire racks to cool completely.

EACH BAR: ABOUT 105 CALORIES | 1G PROTEIN | 19G CARBOHYDRATE | 3G TOTAL FAT (2G SATURATED) | 1G FIBER | 15MG CHOLESTEROL | 80MG SODIUM

FRANGIPANE-APRICOT BARS

These layered bars are sure to be on everyone's most-requested list. They would be equally delicious with cherry or any other favorite jam.

ACTIVE TIME: 45 MINUTES · **TOTAL TIME:** 1 HOUR 25 MINUTES PLUS COOLING
MAKES: 32 BARS

SHORTBREAD CRUST

1½ CUPS ALL-PURPOSE FLOUR

½ CUP CONFECTIONERS' SUGAR

¾ CUP COLD BUTTER (1½ STICKS), CUT INTO PIECES (DO NOT USE MARGARINE)

FRANGIPANE-APRICOT FILLING

1 TUBE OR CAN (7 TO 8 OUNCES) ALMOND PASTE, CRUMBLED

½ CUP GRANULATED SUGAR

4 TABLESPOONS BUTTER, SOFTENED (DO NOT USE MARGARINE)

¼ TEASPOON SALT

2 LARGE EGGS

2 TEASPOONS VANILLA EXTRACT

¼ CUP ALL-PURPOSE FLOUR

1 CUP APRICOT OR SOUR-CHERRY JAM (ABOUT ONE 12-OUNCE JAR)

⅓ CUP SLICED NATURAL ALMONDS (WITH SKINS)

1 Preheat oven to 375°F. Line 13" by 9" baking pan with foil (see page 14); grease foil.

2 Prepare crust: In medium bowl, with wire whisk, mix flour and confectioners' sugar. With pastry blender or two knives used scissor-fashion, cut in butter until mixture resembles fine crumbs. Press crumbs evenly onto bottom of prepared pan. Bake crust until light golden, 16 to 18 minutes. Cool in pan on wire rack.

3 Meanwhile, prepare filling: In large bowl, with mixer at low speed, beat almond paste, granulated sugar, butter, and salt until crumbly. Increase speed to medium, and beat, scraping bowl frequently with rubber spatula, until combined, about 3 minutes (some tiny lumps of almond paste will remain). Beat in eggs and vanilla until smooth. Beat in flour just until combined.

4 Spread jam over cooled crust. Carefully pour almond-paste mixture over jam, spreading with small metal spatula if necessary. Sprinkle top with almonds.

5 Bake until top is light golden, 25 to 30 minutes. Cool completely in pan on wire rack.

6 When cool, lift foil, with pastry, out of pan; peel foil away from sides. Cut lengthwise into 8 strips, then cut each strip crosswise into 4 pieces. Store bars in tightly covered container up to 2 weeks.

EACH BAR: ABOUT 170 CALORIES │ 2G PROTEIN │ 21G CARBOHYDRATE │ 9G TOTAL FAT (4G SATURATED) │ 1G FIBER │ 30MG CHOLESTEROL │ 90MG SODIUM

LATTICE-TOP FIG AND PRUNE BARS

Butter is essential to the texture and flavor of this crust; we don't recommend substituting margarine. The latticework looks fancy, but it is blissfully easy to execute (see Lattices Made Easy, page 100). Kids love to help roll the dough ropes and arrange them on top of the filling.

ACTIVE TIME: 45 MINUTES · **TOTAL TIME:** 1 HOUR 25 MINUTES PLUS CHILLING
MAKES: 24 BARS

COOKIE CRUST

- ¾ CUP BUTTER (1½ STICKS), SOFTENED (DO NOT USE MARGARINE)
- ⅓ CUP GRANULATED SUGAR
- 2 TEASPOONS VANILLA EXTRACT
- 1 LARGE EGG
- 2 CUPS ALL-PURPOSE FLOUR
- ¼ TEASPOON SALT

FIG AND PRUNE FILLING

- 1 PACKAGE (10 OUNCES) CALIMYRNA FIGS
- 1 CUP PITTED PRUNES
- ⅓ CUP PACKED DARK BROWN SUGAR
- 1 CUP WATER
- 2 TABLESPOONS FRESH LEMON JUICE

1 Line 13" by 9" baking pan with foil (see page 14); grease foil.

2 Prepare crust: In large bowl, with mixer at low speed, beat butter and granulated sugar until blended. Increase speed to high; beat until light and creamy, occasionally scraping bowl with rubber spatula. Reduce speed to medium; beat in vanilla and egg. Stir in flour and salt until dough begins to form. With hands, press dough together. Divide dough into two pieces, one slightly larger than the other. Wrap smaller piece in plastic wrap and refrigerate. With hand, press remaining dough evenly onto bottom of prepared pan; refrigerate until ready to use.

3 Prepare filling: With kitchen shears, cut stems from figs. In 2-quart saucepan, cook figs, prunes, brown sugar, and water over medium heat, stirring occasionally, until mixture thickens and most of liquid is absorbed, about 10 minutes. Transfer mixture to food processor with knife blade attached. Add lemon juice and puree until almost smooth. Spoon fig mixture into bowl; cover and refrigerate until cool.

4 Preheat oven to 375°F. Remove dough and filling from refrigerator. With small metal spatula, spread filling evenly over dough in pan; set aside while preparing lattice.

(continued)

5 On lightly floured surface, cut remaining dough into 20 pieces. Roll pieces into ¼-inch-thick ropes. Place half of the ropes diagonally across filling about 1 inch apart; trim ends if necessary. Repeat with remaining ropes at right angles to first ones to make lattice. (If ropes break, just press dough back together.)

6 Bake until crust is golden, about 40 minutes. Cool completely in pan on wire rack.

7 When cool, lift foil, with pastry, out of pan; peel foil away from sides. Cut lengthwise into 4 strips, then cut each strip crosswise into 6 pieces.

TIP To soften butter, let it stand at room temperature. Leave sticks wrapped on counter or unwrapped in a mixing bowl, or cut them into small pieces to speed up the process. Softening can take up to an hour. (Popping cold butter into the microwave is tempting, but zapping can soften it unevenly, creating hot spots, or even melt the butter, in a blink. Then the butter will be too soft to cream properly, which will affect the texture of the brownies or bars.)

EACH BAR: ABOUT 160 CALORIES | 2G PROTEIN | 26G CARBOHYDRATE | 6G TOTAL FAT (4G SATURATED) | 2G FIBER | 24MG CHOLESTEROL | 85MG SODIUM

LATTICES MADE EASY

A lattice topping will make you look like a professional pastry chef, but it is blissfully easy to make. For a simple lattice, place pastry strips about 1 inch apart across the bars, then repeat with an equal number of strips placed at right angles to the first ones to create a lattice design. Turn overhang up over ends of strips; pinch to seal.

A woven lattice is a little more work but the results are eye-catching. Arrange first layer of pastry strips about 1 inch apart across bars as you would do to create a simple lattice; do not seal ends. Fold every other strip back halfway from center. Place center cross strip on bars and replaced folded strips. Now fold back alternate strips; place second cross strip in place. Repeat to weave cross strips into lattice; trim and seal ends.

CHERRY-CHEESECAKE TRIANGLES

If you can't find prepared graham-cracker crumbs, it will take 12 to 13 graham crackers to make the required 1½ cups. Just grind them in the food processor or put them in a plastic bag and pound with a rolling pin.

ACTIVE TIME: 20 MINUTES · **TOTAL TIME:** 1 HOUR 15 MINUTES PLUS COOLING AND CHILLING
MAKES: 16 TRIANGLES

GRAHAM-CRACKER CRUST

1½ CUPS GRAHAM-CRACKER CRUMBS

6 TABLESPOONS BUTTER OR MARGARINE, MELTED

2 TABLESPOONS SUGAR

CHEESE FILLING

1½ PACKAGES (8 OUNCES EACH) LIGHT CREAM CHEESE (NEUFCHÂTEL), SOFTENED

½ CUP SUGAR

2 LARGE EGGS

2 TEASPOONS FRESHLY GRATED LEMON PEEL

1½ TEASPOONS VANILLA EXTRACT

1 CUP CANNED CHERRY-PIE FILLING

1 Preheat oven to 350°F. Line 9-inch square baking pan with foil (see page 14); grease foil.
2 Prepare crust: In small bowl, with fork, stir graham-cracker crumbs, butter, and sugar until blended. With hand, press mixture onto bottom of prepared pan. Bake 10 minutes. Cool completely in pan on wire rack.
3 Prepare filling: In small bowl, with mixer at medium speed, beat cream cheese until smooth. Gradually beat in sugar. Beat in eggs, lemon peel, and vanilla just until blended.
4 Pour cream-cheese mixture evenly over cooled crust. Spoon dollops of cherry-pie filling over cheese mixture. With tip of knife, cut and twist through mixture to create marbled effect.
5 Bake until toothpick inserted in center comes out almost clean, about 45 minutes. Cool completely in pan on wire rack; refrigerate until ready to serve. Then lift foil, with pastry, out of pan; peel foil away from sides. Cut into 4 strips, then cut each strip crosswise into 4 squares.

EACH TRIANGLE: ABOUT 210 CALORIES | 4G PROTEIN | 23G CARBOHYDRATE | 11G TOTAL FAT (4G SATURATED) | 0.5G FIBER | 46MG CHOLESTEROL | 220MG SODIUM

(continued)

Cherry-Cheesecake Triangles (page 101)

EASY CHEESECAKE BROWNIES

A box of brownie mix, a package of cream cheese, and a few other ingredients you're likely to have on hand can be turned into these luscious brownies like magic.

ACTIVE TIME: 25 MINUTES · **TOTAL TIME:** 1 HOUR PLUS COOLING
MAKES: 24 BROWNIES

---

1 BOX (19½ TO 22½ OUNCES) FAMILY-SIZE 13"x9" BROWNIE MIX

1½ PACKAGES (8 OUNCES EACH) COLD CREAM CHEESE

½ CUP SUGAR

1 LARGE EGG

½ TEASPOON VANILLA EXTRACT

1 Preheat oven to 350°F. Line 13" by 9" baking pan with foil (see page 14); grease foil.

2 Prepare brownie mix according to package directions; set aside.

3 In small bowl, with mixer at medium speed, beat cream cheese until smooth; gradually beat in sugar. Beat in egg and vanilla just until blended.

4 Spread 1½ cups brownie batter in prepared pan. Spoon cream cheese mixture in 6 large dollops on top of brownie batter. Spoon remaining brownie batter over and between cream cheese in 6 large dollops. With tip of knife, cut and twist through mixtures to create marbled effect.

5 Bake until toothpick inserted in center comes out almost clean, 35 to 40 minutes. Cool completely in pan on wire rack.

6 When cool, lift foil, with pastry, out of pan; peel foil away from sides. Cut lengthwise into 4 strips, then cut each strip crosswise into 6 pieces.

EACH BROWNIE: ABOUT 216 CALORIES | 4G PROTEIN | 24G CARBOHYDRATE | 12G TOTAL FAT (4G SATURATED) | 1G FIBER | 42MG CHOLESTEROL | 148MG SODIUM

LEMONY CHEESECAKE BITES

Don't skip these! They're a cheesecake lover's dream, with rich, creamy texture and a triple taste of citrus: There's lime in the crust, lemon in the filling, and an orange-flecked sour-cream layer on top.

ACTIVE TIME: 30 MINUTES · **TOTAL TIME:** 1 HOUR 40 MINUTES PLUS COOLING AND CHILLING
MAKES: 64 BITES

VANILLA-WAFER CRUST

5 TABLESPOONS BUTTER OR MARGARINE

¾ TEASPOON FRESHLY GRATED LIME PEEL

1¾ CUPS VANILLA-WAFER COOKIE CRUMBS (ABOUT 48 COOKIES)

LEMON FILLING

2 LARGE LEMONS

1¼ CUPS SUGAR

2 TABLESPOONS CORNSTARCH

4 PACKAGES (8 OUNCES EACH) CREAM CHEESE, SOFTENED

½ CUP HEAVY OR WHIPPING CREAM

5 LARGE EGGS

SOUR-CREAM TOPPING

1½ CUPS SOUR CREAM

3 TABLESPOONS SUGAR

1 TEASPOON FRESHLY GRATED ORANGE PEEL

1 Preheat oven to 350°F. Line 13" by 9" baking pan with foil (see page 14); grease foil. Prepare crust: In 10-inch skillet, melt butter over low heat. Remove from heat and stir in lime peel. With fork, stir in crumbs until crumbs are moistened. With hand, press crumb mixture firmly onto bottom of prepared baking pan. Bake 10 minutes. Cool in pan on wire rack.

2 Prepare filling: From lemons, grate 1 tablespoon peel and squeeze ¼ cup juice. In small bowl, with wire whisk, mix sugar and cornstarch until blended. In large bowl, with mixer at medium speed, beat cream cheese, scraping bowl occasionally with rubber spatula, until smooth, about 5 minutes. Slowly beat in sugar mixture, cream, and lemon juice and peel, scraping bowl often, until blended. At low speed, beat in eggs one at a time just until blended (do not overbeat).

3 Pour filling onto crust: Place medium roasting pan (15½" by 10½") on rack in oven; fill with *1 inch boiling water.* Carefully place cheesecake pan in roasting pan. (Water will come about halfway up side of cheesecake pan.)

(continued)

4 Bake until toothpick inserted 1 inch from center comes out almost clean and center of cheesecake is not completely set, 55 to 60 minutes. Remove cheesecake from oven. Turn off oven.

5 While cheesecake is baking, prepare topping: In small bowl, stir sour cream, sugar, and orange peel until blended; cover and refrigerate until ready to use.

6 After removing cheesecake from oven, spread topping over hot cake. Return cheesecake to oven; heat 5 minutes (oven is off but still hot). Cool cheesecake completely in pan on wire rack. Cover and refrigerate at least 6 hours or overnight.

7 When cold, lift foil, with cheesecake, out of pan; peel foil away from sides. Cut lengthwise into 8 strips; cut each strip crosswise into 8 pieces. Refrigerate leftovers.

EACH BITE: ABOUT 115 CALORIES | 2G PROTEIN | 8G CARBOHYDRATE | 9G TOTAL FAT (5G SATURATED) | 0G FIBER | 41MG CHOLESTEROL | 72MG SODIUM

BAKERY-PERFECT PRESENTATION

Cheesecake tastes better a day or so after it's baked, so for exceptional results, make this recipe up to 2 days ahead. If that's not possible, refrigerate in the pan for at least 6 hours, tightly wrapping it with plastic wrap so the cheesecake does not pick up aromas from other foods in the refrigerator. When you are ready to serve, use a large, sharp knife to cut the bars into squares, as described in step 7. Wipe the blade clean after making each cut, then dip the blade in hot water, dry it off quickly, and make the next cut.

CITRUS BARS

The flavors of orange, lemon, and lime meld beautifully in these sweet, colorful bars.

ACTIVE TIME: 15 MINUTES · **TOTAL TIME:** 30 MINUTES PLUS COOLING
MAKES: 36 BARS

CRUST

1½ CUPS ALL-PURPOSE FLOUR

½ CUP CONFECTIONERS' SUGAR

¾ CUP COLD BUTTER OR MARGARINE (1½ STICKS)

CITRUS FILLING

1 ORANGE

1 LEMON

1 LIME

3 LARGE EGGS

1 CUP GRANULATED SUGAR

3 TABLESPOONS ALL-PURPOSE FLOUR

½ TEASPOON BAKING POWDER

½ TEASPOON SALT

1 TABLESPOON CONFECTIONERS' SUGAR

1 Preheat oven to 350°F. Line 13" by 9" baking pan with foil (see page 14); grease foil.

2 Prepare crust: In medium bowl, with wire whisk, mix flour and confectioners' sugar. With pastry blender or two knives used scissor-fashion, cut in butter until mixture resembles coarse crumbs. With hand, press mixture evenly onto bottom of prepared pan. Bake until lightly browned, 20 to 22 minutes.

3 Meanwhile, prepare filling: Grate ½ teaspoon peel from orange, ½ tea-spoon peel from lemon, and ½ teaspoon peel from lime; squeeze 2 tablespoons juice from each fruit. In large bowl, with mixer at high speed, beat eggs until thick and lemon-colored, about 2 minutes. Reduce speed to low. Add citrus peel, citrus juice, granulated sugar, flour, baking powder, and salt; beat, occasionally scraping bowl with rubber spatula, just until blended. Pour citrus mixture over hot crust.

4 Bake until filling is just set and pale golden around edges, about 15 minutes. Transfer pan to wire rack.

5 Place confectioners' sugar in fine sieve and sprinkle over warm filling. Cool completely in pan on wire rack.

6 When cool, lift foil, with pastry, out of pan; peel away foil from sides. Cut lengthwise into 3 strips, then cut each strip crosswise into 12 bars.

EACH BAR: ABOUT 90 CALORIES | 1G PROTEIN | 12G CARBOHYDRATE | 4G TOTAL FAT (3G SATURATED) | 0G FIBER | 28MG CHOLESTEROL | 78MG SODIUM

FRESH LEMON BARS

A lot of people call lemon bars (also known as lemon squares) "my specialty" and whip them up at the drop of a hat for coffee klatches, bake sales, and potluck suppers. Try this recipe just once and you may join their ranks.

ACTIVE TIME: 15 MINUTES · **TOTAL TIME:** 45 MINUTES PLUS COOLING
MAKES: 36 BARS

1½ CUPS PLUS 3 TABLESPOONS ALL-PURPOSE FLOUR

½ CUP PLUS 1 TABLESPOON CONFECTIONERS' SUGAR

¾ CUP COLD BUTTER OR MARGARINE (1½ STICKS), CUT INTO PIECES

2 LARGE LEMONS (SEE TIP, PAGE 109)

3 LARGE EGGS

1 CUP GRANULATED SUGAR

½ TEASPOON BAKING POWDER

½ TEASPOON SALT

1 Preheat oven to 350°F. Line 13" by 9" baking pan with foil (see page 14); lightly grease foil.

2 In medium bowl, with wire whisk, mix 1½ cups flour and ½ cup confectioners' sugar. With pastry blender or two knives used scissor-fashion, cut in butter until mixture resembles coarse crumbs. Transfer crumb mixture to prepared pan. With floured hand, pat firmly onto bottom of pan. Bake until lightly browned, 15 to 17 minutes.

3 Meanwhile, from lemons, grate 1 teaspoon peel and squeeze ⅓ cup juice. In large bowl, with mixer at high speed, beat eggs until thick and lemon-colored, about 3 minutes. Reduce mixer speed to low. Add lemon peel and juice, granulated sugar, baking powder, salt, and remaining 3 tablespoons flour; beat, scraping bowl occasionally with rubber spatula, until blended.

4 Pour lemon filling over warm crust.

5 Return to oven and bake until filling is just set and golden around edges, about 15 minutes. Transfer pan to wire rack. Sift remaining 1 tablespoon confectioners' sugar over warm filling. Cool completely in pan.

6 When cool, lift foil, with pastry, out of pan; peel foil away from sides. Cut lengthwise into 3 strips, then cut each strip crosswise into 12 pieces.

EACH BAR: ABOUT 95 CALORIES | 1G PROTEIN | 12G CARBOHYDRATE | 4G TOTAL FAT (3G SATURATED) | 0G FIBER | 28MG CHOLESTEROL | 85MG SODIUM

TIP To get more juice per lemon (or any citrus fruit), zap citrus whole in the microwave for 20 to 30 seconds. The juice flows more readily when the fruit is warm. Squeeze as you like, either with an electric citrus juicer for big jobs or an old-fashioned reamer for a few tablespoons.

CRANBERRY-CHEESECAKE FINGERS

These treats have just 100 calories each! Cranberry sauce, which gives them their distinctive flavor, is available in supermarkets year-round.

ACTIVE TIME: 30 MINUTES · **TOTAL TIME:** 1 HOUR 20 MINUTES PLUS COOLING AND CHILLING
MAKES: 48 FINGERS

GRAHAM-CRACKER CRUST

2¼ CUPS GRAHAM-CRACKER CRUMBS (OR CRUMBS FROM ABOUT 18 CRACKERS)

½ CUP BUTTER OR MARGARINE (1 STICK), MELTED

3 TABLESPOONS SUGAR

CHEESECAKE FILLING

2 PACKAGES (8 OUNCES EACH) LIGHT CREAM CHEESE (NEUFCHÂTEL), SOFTENED

¾ CUP SUGAR

3 LARGE EGGS

2 TEASPOONS FRESHLY GRATED LEMON PEEL

2 TEASPOONS VANILLA EXTRACT

1 CAN (16 OUNCES) WHOLE-BERRY CRANBERRY SAUCE

1 Preheat oven to 350°F. Line 13" by 9" baking pan with foil (see page 14); grease foil.

2 Prepare crust: In small bowl, with fork, stir graham-cracker crumbs, melted butter, and sugar until blended. With hand, press mixture evenly onto bottom of prepared pan. Bake 10 minutes. Cool completely in pan on wire rack.

3 Prepare filling: In medium bowl, with mixer at medium speed, beat cream cheese, occasionally scraping down bowl with rubber spatula, until smooth; gradually beat in sugar. Beat in eggs, lemon peel, and vanilla just until blended. Pour cream-cheese mixture evenly over cooled crust.

4 In small bowl, stir cranberry sauce to loosen. Spoon dollops of sauce over cream-cheese mixture. With tip of knife, cut and twist through mixture to create marbled effect. See page 15 for photo of technique.

5 Bake until toothpick inserted in center comes out almost clean, 40 to 45 minutes. Cool completely in pan on wire rack. Cover and refrigerate until firm enough to slice, at least 6 hours or overnight. To serve, lift foil, with pastry, out of pan; peel foil away from sides. Cut lengthwise into 6 strips, then cut each strip crosswise into 8 pieces.

EACH FINGER: ABOUT 100 CALORIES | 2G PROTEIN | 11G CARBOHYDRATE | 6G TOTAL FAT (3G SATURATED) | 0G FIBER | 26MG CHOLESTEROL | 85MG SODIUM

LEMON-CRANBERRY SHORTBREAD

Not your grandmother's shortbread, these glazed melt-in-your-mouth bars are festive enough for the holidays and pretty enough for any afternoon tea.

ACTIVE TIME: 30 MINUTES · **TOTAL TIME:** 1 HOUR 5 MINUTES PLUS COOLING
MAKES: 36 BARS

---

2 TO 3 LEMONS

¾ CUP COLD BUTTER (1½ STICKS), CUT INTO PIECES (DO NOT USE MARGARINE)

¼ CUP GRANULATED SUGAR

1½ CUPS CONFECTIONERS' SUGAR

2 CUPS ALL-PURPOSE FLOUR

½ CUP DRIED CRANBERRIES

1 Preheat oven to 300°F. Line 13" by 9" baking pan with foil (see page 14).

2 From lemons, grate 2 tablespoons plus ½ teaspoon peel and squeeze 2 tablespoons plus 1 teaspoon juice.

3 In food processor with knife blade attached, process butter, granulated sugar, ½ cup confectioners' sugar, 2 tablespoons lemon peel, and 1 tablespoon lemon juice until creamy. Add flour and pulse until dough begins to come together. Add cranberries and pulse until evenly mixed into dough (most cranberries will be chopped; a few will remain whole). With fingers, press dough evenly onto bottom of prepared pan.

4 Bake shortbread until edges are lightly browned and top is pale golden, 35 to 40 minutes. Cool in pan on wire rack.

5 When cool, in small bowl, with spoon, stir remaining 1 cup confectioners' sugar, 1 tablespoon lemon juice, and remaining ½ teaspoon lemon peel until smooth. Add more juice to reach a good spreading consistency as needed. Spread glaze evenly over shortbread. Let stand until glaze sets, about 30 minutes.

6 When glaze has set, lift foil, with shortbread, out of pan; peel foil away from sides. Cut lengthwise into 3 strips, then cut each strip crosswise into 12 bars. Store shortbread in tightly covered container, with waxed paper between layers, at room temperature up to 4 days, or in freezer up to 3 months.

EACH BAR: ABOUT 90 CALORIES | 1G PROTEIN | 13G CARBOHYDRATE | 4G TOTAL FAT (3G SATURATED) | 0.5G FIBER | 11MG CHOLESTEROL | 40MG SODIUM

LEMON-AND-GINGER SHORTBREAD TRIANGLES

For a lively twist on traditional shortbread cookies, we added lemon and crystallized ginger.

ACTIVE TIME: 20 MINUTES · **TOTAL TIME:** 50 MINUTES PLUS COOLING
MAKES: 48 TRIANGLES

1	LEMON	½	CUP CRYSTALLIZED GINGER, CHOPPED
¾	CUP BUTTER OR MARGARINE (1½ STICKS), SOFTENED	¼	TEASPOON SALT
¾	CUP GRANULATED SUGAR	1	LARGE EGG
2	CUPS ALL-PURPOSE FLOUR	¾	CUP CONFECTIONERS' SUGAR
⅓	CUP YELLOW CORNMEAL		

1   Preheat oven to 350°F. Line 13" by 9" baking pan with foil (see page 14); grease foil.

2   From lemon, grate 1½ teaspoons peel and squeeze 3 tablespoons juice.

3   In large bowl, with mixer at low speed, beat butter, granulated sugar, and lemon peel until blended. Increase speed to high; beat until light and fluffy, about 2 minutes. Reduce speed to low and beat in flour, cornmeal, ginger, salt, and egg just until blended (mixture will be crumbly). Sprinkle mixture evenly into prepared pan. With hand, pat firmly to form compact layer.

4   Bake until golden around edges and toothpick inserted in center of pan comes out clean, 30 to 35 minutes. Cool completely in pan on wire rack.

5   When shortbread is cool, in small bowl, with wire whisk or fork, mix lemon juice and confectioners' sugar until blended and smooth. Pour glaze over shortbread and, with small metal spatula, spread evenly. Let stand until glaze sets, about 1 hour.

6   When glaze has set, lift foil, with shortbread, out of pan; peel foil away from sides. Cut lengthwise into 4 strips, then cut each strip crosswise into 6 pieces. Cut each piece diagonally in half.

EACH TRIANGLE: ABOUT 75 CALORIES | 1G PROTEIN | 11G CARBOHYDRATE | 3G TOTAL FAT (2G SATURATED) | 0G FIBER | 12MG CHOLESTEROL | 45MG SODIUM

CHOCKFUL OF NUTS

Macadamia Triangles (page 116)

MACADAMIA TRIANGLES

This elegant special-occasion cookie owes its fine flavor to macadamia nuts. Native to Australia, macadamia trees were planted in Hawaii near the end of the nineteenth century. The nuts are a little pricier than others but worth the expense.

ACTIVE TIME: 15 MINUTES · **TOTAL TIME:** 50 MINUTES PLUS COOLING
MAKES: 32 TRIANGLES

---

1 CUP ALL-PURPOSE FLOUR	1 JAR (7 OUNCES) MACADAMIA NUTS
¼ CUP GRANULATED SUGAR	⅔ CUP PACKED LIGHT BROWN SUGAR
⅛ TEASPOON SALT	1 LARGE EGG
6 TABLESPOONS COLD BUTTER OR MARGARINE	2 TEASPOONS VANILLA EXTRACT
3 TABLESPOONS COLD WATER	

1 Preheat oven to 425°F. Line 9-inch square baking pan with foil (see page 14); grease foil

2 In medium bowl, with wire whisk, mix flour, granulated sugar, and salt. With pastry blender or two knives used scissor-fashion, cut in butter until mixture resembles coarse crumbs. Sprinkle in water, 1 tablespoon at a time, mixing lightly with fork after each addition, until dough is just moist enough to hold together.

3 With lightly floured hand, press dough evenly onto bottom of prepared pan. With fork, prick dough at 1-inch intervals. Bake crust until golden, 15 to 20 minutes (crust may crack slightly during baking). Cool completely in pan on wire rack. Turn oven control to 375°F.

4 Coarsely chop ½ cup macadamia nuts; reserve for topping. In food processor with knife blade attached, process remaining macadamia nuts with brown sugar until nuts are finely ground. Add egg and vanilla; pulse until just combined.

5 Spread macadamia filling evenly over cooled crust. Sprinkle reserved chopped macadamia nuts on top. Bake until filling is set, about 20 minutes. Cool completely in pan on wire rack.

6 When cool, lift foil, with pastry, out of pan; peel foil away from sides. Cut into 4 strips, then cut each strip crosswise into 4 squares. Cut each square diagonally in half.

EACH TRIANGLE: ABOUT 105 CALORIES | 1G PROTEIN | 10G CARBOHYDRATE | 7G TOTAL FAT (2G SATURATED) | 1G FIBER | 12MG CHOLESTEROL | 35MG SODIUM

PECAN TRIANGLES

Enjoy the rich flavor of pecan pie in bite-size morsels. Because they keep for up to a week, these are great party make-aheads.

ACTIVE TIME: 30 MINUTES · **TOTAL TIME:** 1 HOUR 15 MINUTES PLUS COOLING
MAKES: 64 TRIANGLES

CRUST

- 3 CUPS ALL-PURPOSE FLOUR
- ¼ CUP GRANULATED SUGAR
- ½ TEASPOON BAKING POWDER
- ½ TEASPOON SALT
- ½ CUP COLD BUTTER OR MARGARINE (1 STICK)
- ½ CUP VEGETABLE SHORTENING

PECAN FILLING

- 1¼ CUPS PACKED LIGHT BROWN SUGAR
- 1 CUP BUTTER OR MARGARINE (2 STICKS)
- ¾ CUP HONEY
- ½ CUP GRANULATED SUGAR
- ¼ CUP HEAVY OR WHIPPING CREAM
- 4 CUPS PECANS (1 POUND), VERY COARSELY CHOPPED
- 1 TABLESPOON VANILLA EXTRACT

1 Preheat oven to 400°F. Line 15½" by 10½" jelly-roll pan with foil (see page 14); grease foil.

2 Prepare crust: In large bowl, with wire whisk, mix flour, granulated sugar, baking powder, and salt. With pastry blender or two knives used scissor-fashion, cut in butter and shortening until mixture resembles fine crumbs. With hand, firmly press crumbs evenly onto bottom and up sides of prepared pan.

3 Bake until golden, 12 to 15 minutes. Remove from oven. Turn oven control to 350°F.

4 While crust is baking, prepare filling: In 3-quart saucepan, heat brown sugar, butter, honey, granulated sugar, and cream to boiling over high heat. Add pecans to sugar mixture and heat to boiling. Remove from heat and stir in vanilla. Carefully pour pecan mixture over warm crust.

5 Bake until edges of filling begin to set (filling will be bubbly and will firm up as pastry cools), about 30 minutes. Cool in pan on wire rack until filling is firm to the touch.

6 When cool, lift foil, with pastry, from pan; peel foil away from sides. Cut lengthwise into 4 strips, then cut each strip crosswise into 8 pieces. Cut each piece diagonally in half.

EACH TRIANGLE: ABOUT 160 CALORIES | 1G PROTEIN | 16G CARBOHYDRATE | 11G TOTAL FAT (3G SATURATED) | 1G FIBER | 5MG CHOLESTEROL | 76MG SODIUM

CARAMEL-PECAN BARS

A tasty trio of pecans, caramel, and chocolate nestles on a sweet, golden pastry crust.

ACTIVE TIME: 1 HOUR · TOTAL TIME: 1 HOUR 25 MINUTES PLUS COOLING AND CHILLING

MAKES: 48 BARS

COOKIE CRUST

¾ CUP BUTTER (1½ STICKS), SOFTENED (DO NOT USE MARGARINE)

¾ CUP CONFECTIONERS' SUGAR

1½ TEASPOONS VANILLA EXTRACT

2¼ CUPS ALL-PURPOSE FLOUR

CARAMEL-PECAN FILLING

1 CUP PACKED BROWN SUGAR

½ CUP HONEY

½ CUP BUTTER (1 STICK), CUT INTO PIECES (DO NOT USE MARGARINE)

⅓ CUP GRANULATED SUGAR

¼ CUP HEAVY OR WHIPPING CREAM

2 TEASPOONS VANILLA EXTRACT

1½ CUPS PECANS (6 OUNCES), TOASTED (PAGE 31) AND COARSELY CHOPPED

2 SQUARES (2 OUNCES) SEMISWEET CHOCOLATE, MELTED

1   Preheat oven to 350°F. Line 13" by 9" baking pan with foil (see page 14); grease foil.

2   Prepare crust: In large bowl, with mixer at medium speed, beat butter, confectioners' sugar, and vanilla until creamy, about 2 minutes. At low speed, gradually beat in flour until mixture resembles fine crumbs. Sprinkle into prepared pan. With hand, firmly pat crumbs evenly onto bottom of pan. Bake crust until lightly browned, 25 to 30 minutes.

3   Prepare filling: In 2-quart saucepan, heat brown sugar, honey, butter, granulated sugar, cream, and vanilla to full rolling boil over high heat, stirring frequently. Reduce heat to medium-high; set candy thermometer in place and continue cooking, without stirring, until temperature reaches 248°F or firm-ball stage (when small amount of mixture dropped into very cold water forms a ball that does not flatten upon removal from water).

4   Sprinkle pecans evenly over warm crust. Pour hot caramel over nuts. Cool in pan on wire rack until caramel is room temperature and has formed a skin on top, about 1 hour.

5   With fork, drizzle melted chocolate over caramel. Cover and refrigerate until pastry is cold and chocolate is set, at least 1 hour. Lift foil, with pastry, out of pan; peel foil away from sides. Cut lengthwise into 6 strips, the cut each strip into 8 pieces.

EACH BAR: ABOUT 140 CALORIES | 1G PROTEIN | 16G CARBOHYDRATE | 8G TOTAL FAT (4G SATURATED) | 1G FIBER | 15MG CHOLESTEROL | 55MG SODIUM

BROWN-SUGAR AND PECAN FINGERS

A shortbread-style dough that's rolled directly onto a cookie sheet, then cut into "fingers" after baking.

ACTIVE TIME: 25 MINUTES · **TOTAL TIME:** 45 MINUTES PLUS COOLING
MAKES: 24 FINGERS

¾ CUP BUTTER OR MARGARINE (1½ STICKS), SOFTENED

⅓ CUP PACKED DARK BROWN SUGAR

¼ CUP GRANULATED SUGAR

1 TEASPOON VANILLA EXTRACT

¼ TEASPOON SALT

1¾ CUPS ALL-PURPOSE FLOUR

½ CUP PECANS, CHOPPED

1 Preheat oven to 350°F. In large bowl, with mixer at medium speed, beat butter, brown and granulated sugars, vanilla, and salt until creamy, about 2 minutes. At low speed, gradually beat in flour until just evenly moistened. With hand, press dough together to form ball.

2 Divide dough in half. On one side of ungreased large cookie sheet, roll half of dough, covered with waxed paper, lengthwise into 12" by 5" rectangle. On other side of same cookie sheet, repeat with remaining dough, 1½ inches from first rectangle. With fork, prick dough at 1-inch intervals. Press tines of fork along long sides of rectangles to form decorative edge. Sprinkle pecans evenly over rectangles; press gently to make nuts adhere.

3 Bake until edges are lightly browned, 20 to 25 minutes. While still warm, cut each rectangle crosswise into 12 finger-shaped cookies. Transfer fingers to wire rack to cool. Store in tightly covered container up to 1 week.

EACH TRIANGLE: ABOUT 120 CALORIES | 1G PROTEIN | 12G CARBOHYDRATE | 8G TOTAL FAT (4G SATURATED) | 0.5G FIBER | 16MG CHOLESTEROL | 90MG SODIUM

CHOCOLATE PECAN BARS

If you have the extra time, toast the pecans in the oven for 5 to 10 minutes (see page 31). Cool before using.

ACTIVE TIME: 25 MINUTES · TOTAL TIME: 1 HOUR PLUS COOLING
MAKES: 32 BARS

CRUST

¾ CUP BUTTER OR MARGARINE (1½ STICKS), SOFTENED

½ CUP CONFECTIONERS' SUGAR

2 CUPS ALL-PURPOSE FLOUR

CHOCOLATE PECAN FILLING

2 SQUARES (2 OUNCES) SEMISWEET CHOCOLATE

2 SQUARES (2 OUNCES) UNSWEETENED CHOCOLATE

2 TABLESPOONS BUTTER OR MARGARINE

⅔ CUP PACKED LIGHT BROWN SUGAR

⅔ CUP DARK CORN SYRUP

3 LARGE EGGS, LIGHTLY BEATEN

1 TEASPOON VANILLA EXTRACT

1½ CUPS PECANS (6 OUNCES), COARSELY CHOPPED

1   Preheat oven to 350°F. Line 13" by 9" baking pan with foil (see page 14).

2   Prepare crust: In medium bowl, with mixer at medium speed, beat butter and confectioners' sugar until combined. Reduce speed to low and beat in flour until combined. With lightly floured hand, press dough evenly onto bottom and 1 inch up side of prepared pan. Line pan with foil and fill with pie weights or dry beans. Bake until lightly golden, 15 to 20 minutes. Cool to room temperature on wire rack; remove foil with weights.

3   Meanwhile, prepare filling: In 3-quart saucepan, melt semisweet and unsweetened chocolates and butter over very low heat. Cool to lukewarm. With rubber spatula, stir in brown sugar and corn syrup until smooth. Stir in eggs, vanilla, and pecans. Pour filling over baked crust.

4   Bake until filling is set, about 30 minutes longer. Cool completely in pan on wire rack.

5   When cool, lift foil, with pastry, out of pan; peel foil away from sides. Cut lengthwise into 4 strips, then cut each strip crosswise into 8 pieces.

EACH BAR: ABOUT 175 CALORIES | 2G PROTEIN | 20G CARBOHYDRATE | 10G TOTAL FAT (4G SATURATED) | 1G FIBER | 34MG CHOLESTEROL | 70MG SODIUM

PECAN-CARAMEL BROWNIE CUPS

These sweet treats are presented in mini muffin cups.

ACTIVE TIME: 40 MINUTES · TOTAL TIME: 10 MINUTES PLUS COOLING AND CHILLING
MAKES: 36 BROWNIE CUPS

18 INDIVIDUALLY WRAPPED ROUND CARAMELS

36 MINI FLUTED FOIL OR PAPER BAKING-CUP LINERS

½ CUP BUTTER OR MARGARINE (1 STICK)

3 SQUARES (3 OUNCES) UNSWEETENED CHOCOLATE, CHOPPED

1 CUP SUGAR

1 TEASPOON VANILLA EXTRACT

2 LARGE EGGS

½ CUP ALL-PURPOSE FLOUR

¼ TEASPOON SALT

36 PECAN HALVES

1 BAR (1 TO 2 OUNCES) MILK CHOCOLATE, BROKEN INTO PIECES

1   Preheat oven to 350°F. Unwrap caramels and cut each horizontally in half. Line 36 mini muffin-pan cups with fluted foil or paper liners. (Make sure to use liners in muffin-pan cups; brownies will stick to pan, even if well greased.)

2   In large microwave-safe bowl, melt butter and unsweetened chocolate in microwave oven on High 1 minute; stir until smooth. Add sugar, vanilla, and eggs and whisk until blended. Whisk in flour and salt until smooth. Spoon batter by rounded measuring teaspoons into prepared muffin-pan cups. Top each with a caramel half and a pecan half.

3   Bake until brownies are firm when lightly pressed, 10 to 12 minutes. Cool brownies in pan on wire rack 10 minutes. Remove from pan and cool completely on rack.

4   In microwave-safe cup, melt milk chocolate in microwave oven on High 45 seconds; stir until smooth. Cool slightly.

5   Place brownie cups on cookie sheet lined with wax paper. Pour milk chocolate into small zip-tight plastic bag. Snip 1 corner of bag to make $\frac{1}{16}$-inch opening and drizzle chocolate over brownie cups. Refrigerate cups until chocolate is set, about 30 minutes. Store brownie cups in tightly covered container, with waxed paper between layers, at room temperature up to 1 week, or in freezer up to 3 months.

EACH BROWNIE CUP: ABOUT 110 CALORIES | 1G PROTEIN | 12G CARBOHYDRATE | 7G TOTAL FAT (3G SATURATED) | 1G FIBER | 19MG CHOLESTEROL | 60MG SODIUM

HAZELNUT BROWNIES

Nutella is a chocolate-hazelnut spread that was created in Italy in the 1940s by Pietro Ferrero. At that time, chocolate was in short supply due to the war, so he stretched what he had by adding ground hazelnuts, creating a spread that became hugely popular. It now can be found in supermarkets, usually near the peanut butter. Try it on toast for a breakfast treat.

ACTIVE TIME: 30 MINUTES · TOTAL TIME: 55 MINUTES PLUS COOLING

MAKES: 24 BROWNIES

1 CUP ALL-PURPOSE FLOUR	1½ CUPS NUTELLA OR OTHER CHOCOLATE-HAZELNUT SPREAD (ABOUT HALF 13-OUNCE JAR)
½ TEASPOON SALT	
¾ CUP BUTTER OR MARGARINE (1½ STICKS)	1½ CUPS SUGAR
4 SQUARES (4 OUNCES) UNSWEETENED CHOCOLATE	1 TEASPOON VANILLA EXTRACT
	4 LARGE EGGS, LIGHTLY BEATEN
2 SQUARES (2 OUNCES) SEMISWEET CHOCOLATE	1 CUP HAZELNUTS (4 OUNCES), TOASTED (PAGE 31) AND COARSELY CHOPPED

1 Preheat oven to 350°F. Line 13" by 9" baking pan with foil (see page 14); grease foil. In small bowl, with wire whisk, mix flour and salt.

2 In 3-quart saucepan, melt butter and unsweetened and semisweet chocolates over low heat, stirring frequently, until smooth. Remove from heat; stir in chocolate-hazelnut spread. Add sugar and vanilla; stir until well blended. Add eggs; stir until well mixed. Stir in flour mixture and nuts, just until blended. Spread batter evenly in prepared pan.

3 Bake until toothpick inserted 2 inches from edge comes out almost clean, 25 to 30 minutes. Cool in pan on wire rack.

4 When cool, lift foil, with brownie, out of pan; peel foil away from sides. Cut brownie lengthwise into 4 strips, then cut each strip crosswise into 6 pieces.

EACH BROWNIE: ABOUT 230 CALORIES | 4G PROTEIN | 23G CARBOHYDRATE | 15G TOTAL FAT (6G SATURATED) | 2G FIBER | 52MG CHOLESTEROL | 125MG SODIUM

EASY HAZELNUT BROWNIES

Want to sink your teeth into a hazelnut brownie fast? Boxed Brownie mix is your ally.

ACTIVE TIME: 15 MINUTES · **TOTAL TIME:** 40 MINUTES PLUS COOLING

MAKES: 24 BROWNIES

---

1   BOX (19½ TO 22½ OUNCES) FAMILY-SIZE 13"x9" BROWNIE MIX

1   CUP HAZELNUTS (4 OUNCES), TOASTED (PAGE 31) AND COARSELY CHOPPED

½   CUP NUTELLA OR OTHER CHOCOLATE-HAZELNUT SPREAD (ABOUT HALF 13-OUNCE JAR; SEE PAGE 123)

1   Preheat oven to 350°F. Line 13" by 9" baking pan with foil (see page 14); grease foil.

2   Prepare brownie mix according to package directions. Stir in hazelnuts and chocolate-hazelnut spread until blended. Spread batter evenly in prepared pan.

3   Bake until toothpick inserted 2 inches from edge comes out almost clean, 25 to 30 minutes. Cool in pan on wire rack.

4   When cool, lift foil, with brownie, out of pan; peel foil away from sides. Cut brownie lengthwise into 4 strips, then cut each strip crosswise into 6 pieces.

EACH BROWNIE: ABOUT 225 CALORIES | 3G PROTEIN | 26G CARBOHYDRATE | 13G TOTAL FAT (2G SATURATED) | 2G FIBER | 18MG CHOLESTEROL | 107MG SODIUM

PEANUT BUTTER SWIRL BROWNIES

For the prettiest swirls, twist the knife through the batters just enough to create a bold pattern. For a photo and tips on technique, see page 15.

ACTIVE TIME: 30 MINUTES · TOTAL TIME: 1 HOUR PLUS COOLING
MAKES: 24 BROWNIES

BROWNIE

1¼ CUPS ALL-PURPOSE FLOUR

¾ TEASPOON BAKING POWDER

½ TEASPOON SALT

½ CUP BUTTER OR MARGARINE (1 STICK)

4 SQUARES (4 OUNCES) UNSWEETENED CHOCOLATE

4 SQUARES (4 OUNCES) SEMISWEET CHOCOLATE

1½ CUPS SUGAR

4 LARGE EGGS, LIGHTLY BEATEN

2 TEASPOONS VANILLA EXTRACT

PEANUT BUTTER SWIRL

1 CUP CREAMY PEANUT BUTTER

4 TABLESPOONS BUTTER OR MARGARINE, SOFTENED

⅓ CUP SUGAR

2 TABLESPOONS ALL-PURPOSE FLOUR

1 LARGE EGG

1 TEASPOON VANILLA EXTRACT

1   Preheat oven to 350°F. Line 13" by 9" baking pan with foil (see page 14); grease foil.

2   Prepare brownie: In small bowl, with wire whisk, mix flour, baking powder, and salt. In 3-quart saucepan, melt butter and chocolates over low heat, stirring often, until smooth. Remove from heat; stir in sugar. Add eggs and vanilla; mix well. Stir flour mixture into chocolate mixture.

3   Prepare peanut butter swirl: In medium bowl, with mixer at medium speed, beat all ingredients until well blended.

4   Spread 2 cups chocolate batter evenly in prepared pan; top with 6 large dollops of peanut butter mixture. Spoon remaining chocolate batter over and between peanut butter in 6 large dollops. With tip of knife, cut and twist through mixtures to create swirled effect.

5   Bake until toothpick inserted 2 inches from edge comes out almost clean, 30 to 35 minutes. Cool completely in pan on wire rack.

6   When cool, lift foil, with brownie, out of pan; peel foil away from sides. Cut brownie lengthwise into 4 strips, then cut each strip crosswise into 6 pieces.

EACH BROWNIE: ABOUT 265 CALORIES | 6G PROTEIN | 26G CARBOHYDRATE | 17G TOTAL FAT
(8G SATURATED) | 2G FIBER | 61MG CHOLESTEROL | 185MG SODIUM

EASY PEANUT BUTTER SWIRL BROWNIES

Irresistible to kids and grownups alike.

ACTIVE TIME: 15 MINUTES · **TOTAL TIME:** 45 MINUTES PLUS COOLING
MAKES: 24 BROWNIES

- 1 BOX (19½ TO 22½ OUNCES) FAMILY-SIZE 13"x9" BROWNIE MIX
- 1 CUP CREAMY PEANUT BUTTER
- 4 TABLESPOONS BUTTER OR MARGARINE

- ⅓ CUP SUGAR
- 2 TABLESPOONS ALL-PURPOSE FLOUR
- 1 LARGE EGG
- 1 TEASPOON VANILLA EXTRACT

1 Preheat oven to 350°F. Line 13" by 9" baking pan with foil (see page 14); grease foil.

2 Prepare brownie mix according to package directions. Set brownie batter aside.

3 In medium bowl, with mixer at medium speed, beat peanut butter, butter, sugar, flour, egg, and vanilla until well blended and smooth.

4 Spread 1½ cups brownie batter evenly in prepared pan. Top with 6 large dollops of peanut-butter mixture. Spoon remaining brownie batter over and between peanut-butter mixture in 6 large dollops. With tip of knife, cut and twist through mixtures to create swirled effect.

5 Bake until toothpick inserted 2 inches from edge comes out almost clean, 30 to 35 minutes. Cool completely in pan on wire rack.

6 When cool, lift foil, with brownie, out of pan; peel foil away from sides. Cut brownie lengthwise into 4 strips, then cut each strip crosswise into 6 pieces.

EACH BROWNIE: ABOUT 244 CALORIES | 5G PROTEIN | 25G CARBOHYDRATE | 15G TOTAL FAT (4G SATURATED) | 1.5G FIBER | 32MG CHOLESTEROL | 176MG SODIUM

PLENTY-OF-PEANUTS BARS

Chocolate, peanuts, and peanut butter combine to make a decadently delicious bar. For an extra-special treat, cut them into twelve or sixteen rectangles and sandwich a generous scoop of vanilla ice cream between two of them.

ACTIVE TIME: 30 MINUTES · **TOTAL TIME:** 1 HOUR 25 MINUTES PLUS COOLING

MAKES: 48 BARS

- ⅓ CUP QUICK-COOKING OATS, UNCOOKED
- 1⅔ CUPS ALL-PURPOSE FLOUR
- ⅓ CUP PLUS 1½ CUPS PACKED LIGHT BROWN SUGAR
- ½ CUP BUTTER OR MARGARINE (1 STICK), SOFTENED
- 3 TABLESPOONS PLUS ⅓ CUP CHUNKY PEANUT BUTTER
- 3 LARGE EGGS
- 4½ TEASPOONS LIGHT MOLASSES
- 2 TEASPOONS BAKING POWDER
- ½ TEASPOON SALT
- 1 CUP SALTED COCKTAIL PEANUTS, (4 OUNCES) CHOPPED
- 1 PACKAGE (6 OUNCES) SEMISWEET CHOCOLATE CHIPS (1 CUP)
- CONFECTIONERS' SUGAR (OPTIONAL)

1 Preheat oven to 350°F. Line 13" by 9" baking pan with foil (see page 14); grease foil.

2 In large bowl, with mixer at low speed, beat oats, 1 cup flour, ⅓ cup brown sugar, 4 tablespoons butter, and 3 tablespoons peanut butter until blended. Pat dough evenly onto bottom of prepared pan and bake 15 minutes.

3 Meanwhile, in large bowl, with mixer at medium speed, beat eggs, molasses, remaining 1½ cups brown sugar, remaining ⅓ cup peanut butter, and remaining 4 tablespoons butter, constantly scraping bowl with rubber spatula, until well combined. Reduce speed to low. Add baking powder, salt, and remaining ⅔ cup flour and beat, occasionally scraping bowl, until blended. With spoon, stir in peanuts and chocolate chips. Spread mixture evenly over hot crust.

4 Bake until golden, about 40 minutes longer. Cool completely in pan on wire rack.

5 When cool, sprinkle with confectioners' sugar, if you like. Lift foil, with pastry, out of pan; peel foil away from sides. Cut lengthwise into 4 strips, then cut each strip crosswise into 12 pieces.

EACH BAR: ABOUT 125 CALORIES | 3G PROTEIN | 16G CARBOHYDRATE | 6G TOTAL FAT (2G SATURATED) | 1G FIBER | 18MG CHOLESTEROL | 94MG SODIUM

PEANUT BUTTER ROCKY-ROAD BARS

All dressed up in toasted marshmallows, peanuts, and chocolate, these peanut butter blondies definitely have more fun. If you have trouble cutting them into bars because of the sticky marshmallow, moisten the knife blade frequently.

ACTIVE TIME: 15 MINUTES · **TOTAL TIME:** 40 MINUTES PLUS COOLING
MAKES: 24 BARS

¾ CUP PACKED LIGHT BROWN SUGAR

⅔ CUP CREAMY PEANUT BUTTER

½ CUP GRANULATED SUGAR

4 TABLESPOONS BUTTER OR MARGARINE, SOFTENED

1¼ CUPS ALL-PURPOSE FLOUR

1 TEASPOON BAKING POWDER

1 TEASPOON VANILLA EXTRACT

2 LARGE EGGS

1 CUP MINIATURE MARSHMALLOWS

½ CUP SALTED COCKTAIL PEANUTS, CHOPPED

½ CUP SEMISWEET CHOCOLATE CHIPS

1 Preheat oven to 350°F. Line 13" by 9" baking pan with foil (see page 14); grease foil.

2 In large bowl, with mixer at low speed, beat brown sugar, peanut butter, granulated sugar, and butter until blended. Increase speed to high; beat until creamy. At low speed, beat in flour, baking powder, vanilla, and eggs, constantly scraping bowl with rubber spatula, until well blended. With hand, press dough evenly onto bottom of prepared pan.

3 Bake 20 minutes. Sprinkle with marshmallows, peanuts, and chocolate chips. Continue baking until golden, about 5 minutes longer. Cool completely in pan on wire rack.

4 When cool, lift foil, with pastry, from pan; peel foil away from sides. Cut lengthwise into 4 strips, then cut each strip crosswise into 6 pieces.

EACH BAR: ABOUT 175 CALORIES | 4G PROTEIN | 22G CARBOHYDRATE | 8G TOTAL FAT (2G SATURATED) | 2G FIBER | 23MG CHOLESTEROL | 94MG SODIUM

TIN ROOF PUFFED RICE TREATS

These nostalgic cereal treats celebrate the sweet-salty combination featured in tin roof sundaes, a chocolate sundae topped with salted, red-skinned Spanish peanuts popular in the early twentieth century.

TOTAL TIME: 40 MINUTES

MAKES: 16 TREATS

½ CUP CREAMY PEANUT BUTTER

24 LARGE MARSHMALLOWS (5 TO 6 OUNCES)

4 CUPS PUFFED RICE CEREAL

4 OUNCES SEMI-SWEET CHOCOLATE CHIPS (⅔ CUP)

2 TABLESPOONS ROASTED, SALTED SPANISH PEANUTS, CHOPPED

1 Spray 8" by 8" baking pan with nonstick cooking spray.

2 In microwave-safe 4-quart bowl, combine peanut butter and marshmallows. Cover bowl with vented plastic wrap and cook in microwave on High 1 minute, until melted. With a rubber spatula, quickly stir in puffed rice until evenly coated. Evenly pat puffed rice mixture into prepared baking pan.

3 In cup, heat chocolate in microwave on High 35 to 45 seconds, until soft; stir until smooth. With offset spatula, spread melted chocolate on top of puffed rice mixture. Sprinkle with peanuts; gently press nuts to adhere.

4 Refrigerate 30 minutes, or until chocolate is set. Cut lengthwise into 4 strips, then cut each strip crosswise into 4 pieces.

EACH TREAT: ABOUT 134 CALORIES | 3G PROTEIN | 18G CARBOHYDRATE | 7G TOTAL FAT (2G SATURATED) | 1G FIBER | 0MG CHOLESTEROL | 50MG SODIUM

PEANUT BUTTER AND JELLY BARS

What kid wouldn't love peanut butter bars sandwiched with a layer of jelly?

ACTIVE TIME: 20 MINUTES · **TOTAL TIME:** 50 MINUTES PLUS COOLING
MAKES: 42 BARS

---

1   CUP SUGAR

1   CUP CREAMY PEANUT BUTTER

½   CUP BUTTER OR MARGARINE (1 STICK), SOFTENED

2   TEASPOONS VANILLA EXTRACT

1   LARGE EGG

2   CUPS ALL-PURPOSE FLOUR

1½   CUPS OLD-FASHIONED OR QUICK-COOKING OATS, UNCOOKED

½   TEASPOON BAKING SODA

1   JAR (12 TO 13 OUNCES) FAVORITE JELLY, JAM, OR PRESERVES (ABOUT 1 CUP)

1 Preheat oven to 350°F. Line 15½" by 10½" jelly-roll pan with foil (see page 14). In large bowl, with mixer at medium speed, beat sugar, peanut butter, butter, vanilla, and egg until blended. Increase speed to high; beat, scraping bowl occasionally with rubber spatula, until light and fluffy, about 1 minute. Reduce speed to low. Add flour, oats, and baking soda and beat just until blended.

2 Transfer 4 cups peanut butter mixture to prepared pan. With fingers, firmly press mixture evenly onto bottom of pan. Spread evenly with jelly, leaving ¼-inch border all around. Sprinkle remaining peanut butter mixture over jelly.

3 Bake until top is lightly browned, 30 to 35 minutes. Cool completely in pan on wire rack.

4 When cool, lift foil, with pastry, out of pan; peel foil away from sides. Cut lengthwise into 6 strips, then cut each strip crosswise into 7 bars.

EACH BAR: ABOUT 145 CALORIES | 3G PROTEIN | 20G CARBOHYDRATE | 6G TOTAL FAT (2G SATURATED) | 1G FIBER | 11MG CHOLESTEROL | 70MG SODIUM

ALMOND CHEESECAKE SWIRL BROWNIES

These sinfully rich brownies are marbled with a ribbon of cheesecake. See page 15 for photo of technique.

ACTIVE TIME: 30 MINUTES · **TOTAL TIME:** 1 HOUR 5 MINUTES PLUS COOLING
MAKES: 24 BROWNIES

1¼ CUPS ALL-PURPOSE FLOUR

¾ TEASPOON BAKING POWDER

½ TEASPOON SALT

½ CUP BUTTER OR MARGARINE (1 STICK)

4 SQUARES (4 OUNCES) UNSWEETENED CHOCOLATE, CHOPPED

4 SQUARES (4 OUNCES) SEMISWEET CHOCOLATE, CHOPPED

2 CUPS SUGAR

5 LARGE EGGS

2½ TEASPOONS VANILLA EXTRACT

1½ PACKAGES (8 OUNCES EACH) COLD CREAM CHEESE

¾ TEASPOON ALMOND EXTRACT

1 Preheat oven to 350°F. Line 13" by 9" baking pan with foil (see page 14); grease foil. In small bowl, with wire whisk, mix flour, baking powder, and salt.

2 In heavy 4-quart saucepan, melt butter and unsweetened and semisweet chocolates over low heat, stirring, until smooth. Remove from heat. With wooden spoon, beat in 1½ cups sugar. Stir in 4 eggs and 2 teaspoons vanilla; beat until well blended. Stir in flour mixture just until blended.

3 In small bowl, with mixer at medium speed, beat cream cheese until smooth; gradually beat in remaining ½ cup sugar. Beat in remaining 1 egg, almond extract, and remaining ½ teaspoon vanilla just until blended.

4 Spread 1½ cups chocolate batter in prepared pan. Spoon cream-cheese mixture in 6 large dollops on top of chocolate mixture (cream-cheese mixture will cover most of chocolate batter). Spoon remaining chocolate batter over and between cream cheese in 6 large dollops. With tip of knife, cut and twist through mixtures to create marbled effect.

5 Bake until toothpick inserted in center comes out almost clean, 35 to 40 minutes. Cool completely in pan on wire rack.

6 When cool, lift foil, with brownie, out of pan; peel foil away from sides. Cut lengthwise into 4 strips, then cut each strip crosswise into 6 pieces.

EACH BROWNIE: ABOUT 238 CALORIES | 4G PROTEIN | 26G CARBOHYDRATE) | 14G TOTAL FAT (8G SATURATED) | 1G FIBER | 70MG CHOLESTEROL | 159MG SODIUM

APRICOT-ALMOND SQUARES

Fruit and nuts are always a popular combination, especially when they come with a sweet pastry crust.

ACTIVE TIME: 30 MINUTES · **TOTAL TIME:** 1 HOUR 55 MINUTES PLUS COOLING
MAKES: 54 SQUARES

APRICOT FILLING

2   CUPS DRIED APRICOTS (12 OUNCES)

½   CUP GRANULATED SUGAR

2½ CUPS WATER

SWEET PASTRY

2   CUPS ALL-PURPOSE FLOUR

½   CUP CONFECTIONERS' SUGAR

¼   TEASPOON SALT

½   CUP COLD BUTTER OR MARGARINE (1 STICK), CUT INTO PIECES

¼   CUP VEGETABLE SHORTENING

3 TO 4 TABLESPOONS ICE WATER

ALMOND TOPPING

1   TUBE OR CAN (7 TO 8 OUNCES) ALMOND PASTE, CRUMBLED

¾   CUP GRANULATED SUGAR

½   CUP BUTTER OR MARGARINE (1 STICK), SOFTENED

3   LARGE EGGS

⅓   CUP ALL-PURPOSE FLOUR

1   TEASPOON VANILLA EXTRACT

⅛   TEASPOON SALT

2   TABLESPOONS CONFECTIONERS' SUGAR

1 Prepare filling: In 2-quart saucepan, heat apricots, sugar, and water to boiling over high heat. Reduce heat to medium-low and cook, uncovered, until apricots are very tender, about 20 minutes. Remove from heat. With potato masher or fork, mash apricots with liquid in saucepan until mixture becomes a thick paste. Cool completely.

2 Meanwhile, prepare pastry: Preheat oven to 350°F. Line 15½" by 10½" jelly-roll pan with foil (see page 14). In medium bowl, with wire whisk, mix flour, confectioners' sugar, and salt. With pastry blender or two knives used scissor-fashion, cut in butter and shortening until mixture resembles coarse crumbs. Sprinkle ice water, 1 tablespoon at a time, into flour mixture, mixing lightly with fork after each addition, until dough is just moist enough to hold together.

3 With hands, press dough evenly onto bottom of prepared jelly-roll pan. Bake until golden brown, 25 to 30 minutes. Cool completely on wire rack.

4 Meanwhile, prepare topping: In food processor with knife blade attached, pulse almond paste, granulated sugar, and butter until mixture is crumbly. Add eggs and pulse, scraping bowl with rubber spatula if necessary, until smooth. Add flour, vanilla, and salt; pulse just until combined.

5 Spread cooled apricot filling evenly over cooled pastry. Pour topping evenly over filling. Bake until top is golden, 40 to 45 minutes. Cool completely in pan on wire rack.

6 Sprinkle top with confectioners' sugar. Lift foil, with pastry, out of pan; peel foil away from sides. Cut lengthwise into 6 strips, then cut each strip crosswise into 9 squares.

EACH SQUARE: ABOUT 125 CALORIES | 2G PROTEIN | 17G CARBOHYDRATE | 6G TOTAL FAT (3G SATURATED) | 1G FIBER | 22MG CHOLESTEROL | 60MG SODIUM

TRIPLE-LAYER ALMOND SHORTBREAD BROWNIES

Trufflelike cake is nestled in a rich shortbread crust, with a semisweet chocolate glaze on top.

ACTIVE TIME: 1 HOUR · TOTAL TIME: 1 HOUR 40 MINUTES PLUS COOLING
MAKES: 72 BROWNIES

---

1   CUP WHOLE NATURAL ALMONDS (4 OUNCES), TOASTED (PAGE 31)

¾   CUP CONFECTIONERS' SUGAR

1¾ CUPS BUTTER OR MARGARINE (3½ STICKS), SOFTENED

¼   TEASPOON ALMOND EXTRACT

2¾ CUPS ALL-PURPOSE FLOUR

5   SQUARES (5 OUNCES) UNSWEETENED CHOCOLATE

3   LARGE EGGS

2   CUPS GRANULATED SUGAR

¼   TEASPOON SALT

2   TEASPOONS VANILLA EXTRACT

6   SQUARES (6 OUNCES) SEMISWEET CHOCOLATE

⅓   CUP HEAVY OR WHIPPING CREAM

½   CUP SLICED ALMONDS, TOASTED (PAGE 31)

---

1   Preheat oven to 350°F. Line 15½" by 10½" jelly-roll pan with foil (see page 14).

2   In food processor with knife blade attached, process whole almonds with ¼ cup confectioners' sugar until nuts are finely ground.

3   In large bowl, with mixer at low speed, beat ¾ cup butter (1½ sticks) and remaining ½ cup confectioners' sugar until blended. Increase speed to high; beat until creamy. At low speed, beat in ground-almond mixture, almond extract, and 1¾ cups flour just until blended (dough will be stiff).

4   With hands, pat dough evenly onto bottom of prepared pan. Bake until golden, 20 to 25 minutes. Cool in pan on wire rack.

5   Meanwhile, in heavy 2-quart saucepan, heat unsweetened chocolate and remaining 1 cup butter (2 sticks) over low heat, stirring frequently, until melted. Remove from heat. Cool slightly, about 10 minutes.

6   In large bowl, with mixer at high speed, beat eggs, granulated sugar, salt, and 1 teaspoon vanilla until ribbon forms when beaters are lifted, 5 to 10 minutes. Beat in chocolate mixture until blended. With spoon, stir in remaining 1 cup flour. Pour chocolate mixture over shortbread crust; spread evenly to edges. Bake until toothpick inserted 1 inch from edge comes out almost clean, 20 to 25 minutes. Cool in pan on wire rack.

BEATING EGGS TO A RIBBON

Whole eggs have been beaten sufficiently if a ribbon forms when the beaters are lifted.

7 In heavy 2-quart saucepan, heat semisweet chocolate and heavy cream over low heat, stirring frequently, until chocolate has melted. Remove from heat; stir in remaining 1 teaspoon vanilla.

8 When cool, lift foil, with brownie, out of pan; peel foil away from sides. With metal spatula, spread chocolate glaze evenly over brownie. Sprinkle sliced almonds on top. Let stand until set, about 2 hours, or refrigerate 30 minutes. Cut lengthwise into 6 strips, then cut each strip crosswise into 12 pieces.

EACH BROWNIE: ABOUT 125 CALORIES │ 2G PROTEIN │ 13G CARBOHYDRATE) │ 8G TOTAL FAT (4G SATURATED) │ 1G FIBER │ 22MG CHOLESTEROL │ 56MG SODIUM

EASY ALMOND SHORTBREAD BROWNIES

These tempting triple-layer bars are easier than they look.

ACTIVE TIME: 35 MINUTES · TOTAL TIME: 1 HOUR 10 MINUTES PLUS COOLING

MAKES: 72 BROWNIES

1 CUP WHOLE NATURAL ALMONDS (4 OUNCES), TOASTED (PAGE 31)	1 BOX (19½ TO 22½ OUNCES) FAMILY-SIZE 13"X9" BROWNIE MIX
¾ CUP CONFECTIONERS' SUGAR	6 SQUARES (6 OUNCES) SEMISWEET CHOCOLATE, CHOPPED
¾ CUP BUTTER OR MARGARINE (1½ STICKS), SOFTENED	⅓ CUP HEAVY OR WHIPPING CREAM
1¾ CUPS ALL-PURPOSE FLOUR	1 TEASPOON VANILLA EXTRACT
¼ TEASPOON ALMOND EXTRACT	½ CUP SLICED ALMONDS, TOASTED

1   Preheat oven to 350°F. Line 15½" by 10½" jelly-roll pan with foil (see page 14).

2   In blender or in food processor with knife blade attached, process whole almonds with ¼ cup confectioners' sugar until nuts are finely ground.

3   In large bowl, with mixer at low speed, beat butter and remaining ½ cup confectioners' sugar until blended. Increase speed to high and beat mixture until light and fluffy. Reduce speed to low; beat in ground almond mixture, flour, and almond extract just until blended.

4   With hand, pat dough evenly onto bottom of prepared pan. Bake until golden, 15 to 20 minutes. Cool in pan on wire rack.

5   Prepare brownie mix according to package directions. Pour batter over shortbread crust and spread evenly. Bake until toothpick inserted near the edge comes out almost clean, 20 to 25 minutes. Cool in pan on wire rack.

6   In medium saucepan, melt semisweet chocolate with cream over low heat, stirring frequently until smooth. Remove from heat; stir in vanilla. With small metal spatula, spread chocolate glaze over brownie. Sprinkle with almonds. Let stand until set, about 2 hours, or refrigerate 30 minutes.

7   When cool, lift foil, with brownie, out of pan; peel foil away from sides. Cut lengthwise into 6 strips, then cut each strip crosswise into 12 pieces.

EACH BROWNIE: ABOUT 110 CALORIES | 2G PROTEIN | 12G CARBOHYDRATE | 7G TOTAL FAT (2G SATURATED) | 1G FIBER | 13MG CHOLESTEROL | 55MG SODIUM

ALMOND LATTICE BROWNIES

A rich almond paste topping is piped over fudgy brownie batter before it is baked.

ACTIVE TIME: 25 MINUTES · TOTAL TIME: 50 MINUTES PLUS COOLING
MAKES: 24 BROWNIES

BROWNIE

1¼ CUPS ALL-PURPOSE FLOUR

½ TEASPOON SALT

½ CUP BUTTER OR MARGARINE (1 STICK)

4 SQUARES (4 OUNCES) SEMISWEET CHOCOLATE

4 SQUARES (4 OUNCES) UNSWEETENED CHOCOLATE

1½ CUPS SUGAR

2 TEASPOONS VANILLA EXTRACT

3 LARGE EGGS, LIGHTLY BEATEN

ALMOND LATTICE TOPPING

1 TUBE OR CAN (7 TO 8 OUNCES) ALMOND PASTE, CRUMBLED

1 LARGE EGG

¼ CUP SUGAR

1 TABLESPOON ALL-PURPOSE FLOUR

1 TEASPOON VANILLA EXTRACT

1 Preheat oven to 350°F. Line 13" by 9" baking pan with foil (see page 14); grease foil.

2 Prepare brownie: In small bowl, with wire whisk, mix flour and salt. In 3-quart saucepan, melt butter and semisweet and unsweetened chocolates over low heat, stirring frequently, until smooth. Remove from heat; stir in sugar and vanilla. Add eggs; stir until well mixed. Stir flour mixture into chocolate mixture just until blended. Spread batter evenly in prepared pan.

3 Prepare topping: In food processor with knife blade attached, pulse all ingredients, scraping bowl with rubber spatula, until mixture is smooth. Transfer almond mixture to small zip-tight plastic bag.

4 With scissors, cut bottom corner of bag on diagonal ¼ inch from edge. Pipe topping over batter to make 10 diagonal lines spaced 1 inch apart. Pipe remaining topping across first set to create a lattice design.

5 Bake until toothpick inserted 2 inches from edge comes out almost clean, 25 to 30 minutes. Cool completely in pan on wire rack.

6 When cool, lift foil, with brownie, out of pan; peel foil away from sides. Cut brownie lengthwise into 4 strips, then cut each strip crosswise into 6 pieces.

EACH BROWNIE: ABOUT 220 CALORIES | 4G PROTEIN | 28G CARBOHYDRATE | 11G TOTAL FAT (5G SATURATED) | 2G FIBER | 46MG CHOLESTEROL | 100MG SODIUM

EASY ALMOND LATTICE BROWNIES

The crisscross design on top looks fancy, but here the brownies are made from time-saving boxed mix.

ACTIVE TIME: 20 MINUTES · **TOTAL TIME:** 45 MINUTES PLUS COOLING
MAKES: 24 BROWNIES

---

1   BOX (19½ TO 22½ OUNCES) FAMILY-SIZE 13"X9" BROWNIE MIX

1   TUBE OR CAN (7 TO 8 OUNCES) ALMOND PASTE, CRUMBLED

1   LARGE EGG

¼   CUP SUGAR

1   TABLESPOON ALL-PURPOSE FLOUR

1   TEASPOON VANILLA EXTRACT

1   Preheat oven to 350°F. Line 13" by 9" baking pan with foil (see page 14); grease foil.

2   Prepare brownie mix according to package directions. Spread batter evenly in prepared pan.

3   In food processor with knife blade attached, pulse almond paste, egg, sugar, flour, and vanilla, scraping bowl with rubber spatula, until mixture is smooth. Transfer almond mixture to small zip-tight plastic bag.

4   With scissors, cut bottom corner of bag on diagonal ¼ inch from edge. Pipe almond topping over brownie batter to make 10 diagonal lines spaced 1 inch apart. Pipe remaining topping diagonally across first set to create a lattice design.

5   Bake until toothpick inserted 2 inches from edge comes out almost clean, 25 to 30 minutes. Cool completely in pan on wire rack.

6   When cool, lift foil, with brownie, out of pan; peel foil away from sides. Cut brownie lengthwise into 4 strips, then cut each strip crosswise into 6 pieces.

EACH BROWNIE: ABOUT 199 CALORIES | 4G PROTEIN | 26G CARBOHYDRATE | 10G TOTAL FAT (1G SATURATED) | 1G FIBER | 26MG CHOLESTEROL | 107MG SODIUM

RASPBERRY-WALNUT STREUSEL BARS

An easy and delicious treat: Raspberry jam is sandwiched between a buttery cookie bottom and a crumbly streusel top.

ACTIVE TIME: 30 MINUTES · TOTAL TIME: 1 HOUR 15 MINUTES PLUS COOLING

MAKES: 24 BARS

¾ CUP BUTTER OR MARGARINE (1½ STICKS), SOFTENED

1 CUP SUGAR

½ TEASPOON FRESHLY GRATED LEMON PEEL

½ TEASPOON GROUND CINNAMON

2 LARGE EGG YOLKS

1 TEASPOON VANILLA EXTRACT

2 CUPS ALL-PURPOSE FLOUR

¼ TEASPOON SALT

1 CUP WALNUTS (4 OUNCES), TOASTED (SEE PAGE 31) AND CHOPPED

½ CUP SEEDLESS RASPBERRY JAM

---

1   Preheat oven to 350°F. Line 9-inch square baking pan with foil (see page 14); grease foil.

2   In large bowl, with mixer at medium speed, beat butter, sugar, lemon peel, and cinnamon, occasionally scraping bowl with rubber spatula, until light and fluffy. Reduce speed to low. Beat in egg yolks and vanilla, frequently scraping bowl, until well combined. Add flour and salt and beat, occasionally scraping bowl, just until blended. With wooden spoon, stir in walnuts (mixture will be crumbly).

3   With lightly floured hand, pat half of dough evenly onto bottom of prepared pan. Spread raspberry jam over dough, leaving ¼-inch border all around. With lightly floured hands, pinch off 1-inch pieces of remaining dough and drop randomly on top of jam (it's okay if dough pieces touch); do not pat.

4   Bake until golden, 45 to 50 minutes. Cool bar completely in pan on wire rack.

5   When cool, lift foil, with pastry, out of pan; peel foil away from sides. Cut into 4 strips, then cut each strip crosswise into 6 pieces.

EACH BAR: ABOUT 176 CALORIES | 2G PROTEIN | 22G CARBOHYDRATE | 10G TOTAL FAT (4G SATURATED) | 1G FIBER | 33MG CHOLESTEROL | 86MG SODIUM

WALNUT TRIANGLES

These triangles are a quick way to make treats for a whole gang. After all, baking a bar in a pan then cutting it into individual servings is a lot easier than rolling, cutting, and baking multiple batches of cookies.

ACTIVE TIME: 25 MINUTES · **TOTAL TIME:** 55 MINUTES PLUS COOLING
MAKES: 32 TRIANGLES

---

5   TABLESPOONS COLD BUTTER OR MARGARINE

1   CUP PLUS 2 TABLESPOONS ALL-PURPOSE FLOUR

1½ CUPS PACKED LIGHT BROWN SUGAR

1   TEASPOON VANILLA EXTRACT

½   TEASPOON SALT

¼   TEASPOON BAKING SODA

2   LARGE EGGS

1   CUP WALNUTS (4 OUNCES), CHOPPED

½   CUP SWEETENED SHREDDED COCONUT

1   Preheat oven to 375°F. Line 9-inch square baking pan with foil (see page 14); grease foil.

2   In medium bowl, with a pastry blender or two knives used scissor-fashion, cut butter into 1 cup flour until mixture resembles fine crumbs. With hand, firmly press crumbs evenly onto bottom of prepared pan. Bake until golden, 10 to 12 minutes. Remove pan from oven.

3   Meanwhile, in another medium bowl, with wire whisk or fork, mix brown sugar, vanilla, salt, baking soda, eggs, and remaining 2 tablespoons flour until blended. With spoon, stir in walnuts and coconut. Spread walnut filling over warm crust.

4   Bake until filling is set and knife inserted 1 inch from edge comes out clean, about 20 minutes. Cool in pan on wire rack until filling is firm to the touch.

5   When cool, lift foil, with pastry, from pan; peel foil away from sides. Cut into 4 strips, then cut each strip crosswise into 4 squares. Cut each square into 2 triangles. Store triangles in tightly covered container up to 1 week.

EACH TRIANGLE: ABOUT 105 CALORIES | 1G PROTEIN | 14G CARBOHYDRATE | 5G TOTAL FAT (1G SATURATED) | 0.5G FIBER | 13MG CHOLESTEROL | 80MG SODIUM

CARAMEL-WALNUT BROWNIES

Ultrarich brownies that have all the flavor of the popular candy known as turtles: nuts, caramel, and chocolate.

ACTIVE TIME: 20 MINUTES · TOTAL TIME: 45 MINUTES PLUS COOLING

MAKES: 24 BROWNIES

---

1 CUP ALL-PURPOSE FLOUR

½ TEASPOON SALT

¾ CUP BUTTER OR MARGARINE (1½ STICKS)

4 SQUARES (4 OUNCES) UNSWEETENED CHOCOLATE

1 CUP GRANULATED SUGAR

1 CUP PACKED LIGHT BROWN SUGAR

3 LARGE EGGS, LIGHTLY BEATEN

1 TEASPOON VANILLA EXTRACT

½ CUP WALNUTS, COARSELY CHOPPED

1 CUP INDIVIDUALLY WRAPPED CARAMELS (ABOUT 25), UNWRAPPED AND EACH CUT IN HALF (SEE TIP)

---

1 Preheat oven to 350°F. Line 13" by 9" baking pan with foil (see page 14); grease foil. In small bowl, with wire whisk, mix flour and salt.

2 In 3-quart saucepan, melt butter and chocolate over low heat, stirring frequently, until smooth. Remove from heat. Stir in granulated and brown sugars and eggs until well mixed, then stir in vanilla. Stir flour mixture into chocolate mixture just until blended; stir in walnuts. Spread batter evenly in prepared pan; sprinkle with caramels.

3 Bake until toothpick inserted 2 inches from edge comes out almost clean, 25 to 30 minutes. Cool completely in pan on wire rack.

4 When cool, lift foil, with brownie, out of pan; peel foil away from sides. Cut lengthwise into 4 strips, then cut each strip crosswise into 6 pieces.

TIP This recipe was tested with several different brands of caramels and, to our surprise, had varying results. For soft, gooey caramels in the baked brownie (our test kitchen's preference) buy a brand that lists sweetened condensed milk as its first ingredient. If you prefer the caramels to be firm and chewy, buy a brand that lists corn syrup or glucose syrup first.

EACH BROWNIE: ABOUT 220 CALORIES | 3G PROTEIN | 28G CARBOHYDRATE | 12G TOTAL FAT (6G SATURATED) | 1G FIBER | 43MG CHOLESTEROL | 140MG SODIUM

WALNUT SHORTBREAD

Here's a shortbread with a delicate nutty flavor.

ACTIVE TIME: 20 MINUTES · **TOTAL TIME:** 45 MINUTES PLUS COOLING

MAKES: 24 COOKIES

½ CUP WALNUTS, TOASTED (PAGE 31)

1½ CUPS ALL-PURPOSE FLOUR

½ CUP SUGAR

½ CUP BUTTER OR MARGARINE (1 STICK), SOFTENED

1   Preheat oven to 325°F. Line 9-inch square baking pan with foil (see page 14). In food processor with knife blade attached, process walnuts with ½ cup flour until nuts are finely ground.

2   In medium bowl, with wire whisk, mix remaining 1 cup flour, sugar, and walnut mixture until blended.

3   With fingertips, blend butter into walnut mixture until well combined and crumbly. With hand, press dough evenly onto bottom of prepared pan.

4   Bake until light golden, 25 to 30 minutes. While still warm, cut shortbread into 4 strips, then cut each strip crosswise into 6 pieces. Cool completely in pan on wire rack.

5   When cool, with small metal spatula, carefully remove shortbread cookies from pan. Lift foil to help loosen shortbread, if necessary.

EACH COOKIE: ABOUT 94 CALORIES | 1G PROTEIN | 11G CARBOHYDRATE | 5G TOTAL FAT (3G SATURATED) | 0.5G FIBER | 10MG CHOLESTEROL | 39MG SODIUM

DECORATIVE TOUCHES

For a kid's over-the-top fantasy or for a more grown-up confection, add one of these to plain brownie or blondie batter:

Candy: Stir up to 1 cup chopped peanut butter cups, malted milk balls, or your favorite candy bar into the batter. (Or sprinkle M&M's or miniature chocolate-covered mints on top just before baking.)

Spice: For a note of sophistication, add ½ teaspoon ground cinnamon, nutmeg, ginger, or a dash of cayenne pepper to the batter.

Dried fruit: Fold in 1 cup chopped dates, apricots, or dried plums—or add whole raisins, cranberries, currants, or tart cherries.

Nuts: Add up to 1 cup unsalted, toasted, chopped nuts. Try unusual varieties such as Brazil nuts or macadamias.

Liqueurs and other liquid flavorings: Stir in 2 tablespoons dark rum or Bourbon, crème de cacao, crème de menthe, coffee liqueur, or almond, orange, or any other fruit- or nut-flavor liqueur. Small amounts (⅛ to ¼ teaspoon) of extracts—such as almond, coconut, peppermint, or rum—are also good.

Mexican Brownies with Coffee Beans or Chopped Semisweet Chocolate (page 56)

CHOCOLATE CURLS

Chocolate curls can turn simple baked goods into special desserts. Shave up a batch of curls and store them in the refrigerator in an airtight container between layers of waxed paper. Use the curls when you want to gussy up a homemade dessert. White chocolate can also be used for curls. Just be very careful when melting it, as it is more delicate than semisweet.

TOTAL TIME: 15 MINUTES PLUS COOLING

---

1   PACKAGE (6 OUNCES) SEMISWEET
    CHOCOLATE CHIPS

2   TABLESPOONS VEGETABLE
    SHORTENING

1 Line 5¾" by 3¼" loaf pan with foil. In heavy 1-quart saucepan, combine chocolate chips and shortening; heat over low heat, stirring frequently, until melted and smooth.

2 Pour chocolate mixture into prepared pan. Refrigerate until chocolate is set, about 2 hours.

3 Remove chocolate from pan by lifting edges of foil. Using vegetable peeler and working over waxed paper, draw blade across surface of chocolate to make large curls. If chocolate is too cold and curls break, let it stand at room temperature until slightly softened, about 30 minutes. Use toothpick or wooden skewer to transfer for garnish.

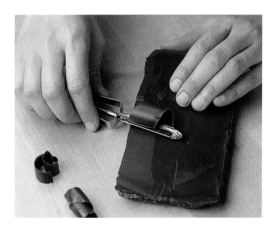

STENCILING

1 Cut lightweight cardboard or manila file folder at least 1 inch larger all around than desired design. With mat knife or single-edge razor blade, cut out stars, triangles, or other shapes of different sizes.

2 Place stencil over unfrosted cake. Sift unsweetened cocoa, confectioners' sugar, or cinnamon-sugar over top. After decoration has been evenly displayed in cutout, carefully lift off stencil to reveal design. Repeat as desired.

THE BEST WAY TO MELT CHOCOLATE

The winning way to melt chocolate? Microwave it. A solid square softens swiftly, and because it's not exposed to direct heat, there's little chance of scorching. Best of all: There's no pot to scrub. To melt masterfully, use a glass measure with an easy-to-grasp handle. Melt chocolate on High just until soft and shiny (it may hold its shape); stir until smooth.

SEMISWEET OR UNSWEETENED CHOCOLATE:
two 1-ounce squares: 1 to 2 minutes
four 1-ounce squares: 1¼ to 2¼ minutes
eight 1-ounce squares: 1½ to 2½ minutes

WHITE CHOCOLATE:
3 ounces: 45 seconds to 1½ minutes
6 ounces: 1¼ to 2¼ minutes

WHITE CHOCOLATE HEARTS

These open designs are very striking when used on dark chocolate bars. They are ideal for Valentine's Day, anniversaries, and Mother's Day.

ACTIVE TIME: 15 MINUTES · TOTAL TIME: 20 MINUTES PLUS SETTING
MAKES: 12 HEARTS

1½ OUNCES WHITE CHOCOLATE,
    SWISS CONFECTIONERY BAR, OR
    WHITE BAKING BAR, COARSELY
    CHOPPED

1 With pencil, draw outline of 12 hearts, each about 1½" by 1½", on piece of waxed paper. Place waxed paper, pencil side down, on cookie sheet; tape to cookie sheet.

2 In top of double boiler set over simmering water, melt white chocolate, stirring, until smooth. Spoon warm chocolate into small pastry bag fitted with small writing tube; use to pipe heart-shaped outlines on waxed paper. Let hearts stand until set.

SMALL-BATCH BUTTER FROSTING

From vanilla to lemon to chocolate, here's a range of frosting flavors that turn already rich brownies into something super-decadent and festive.

TOTAL TIME: 10 MINUTES

MAKES: ABOUT 2⅓ CUPS

---

1 PACKAGE (16 OUNCES) CONFECTIONERS' SUGAR

½ CUP BUTTER OR MARGARINE (1 STICK), SOFTENED

4 TO 6 TABLESPOONS MILK OR HALF-AND-HALF

1½ TEASPOONS VANILLA EXTRACT

In large bowl, with mixer at medium-low speed, beat confectioners' sugar, softened butter, and 3 tablespoons milk until smooth and blended. Beat in additional milk as needed for easy spreading consistency. Increase speed to medium-high; beat until light and fluffy.

EACH TABLESPOON: ABOUT 70 CALORIES | 0G PROTEIN | 12G CARBOHYDRATE | 3G TOTAL FAT (2G SATURATED) | 0G FIBER | 7MG CHOLESTEROL | 25MG SODIUM

LEMON BUTTER FROSTING

Prepare as above but use **2 tablespoons milk, 2 tablespoons fresh lemon juice**, and **1 teaspoon grated lemon peel.** Use only **1 to 2 tablespoons additional milk** as needed for easy spreading consistency.

EACH TABLESPOON: ABOUT 70 CALORIES | 0G PROTEIN | 12G CARBOHYDRATE | 3G TOTAL FAT (2G SATURATED) | 0G FIBER | 7MG CHOLESTEROL | 25MG SODIUM

CHOCOLATE BUTTER FROSTING

Prepare as above but beat in either **4 squares (4 ounces) bittersweet chocolate**, melted and cooled, or **3 squares (3 ounces) semisweet chocolate plus 1 square (1 ounce) unsweetened chocolate**, melted and cooled. Makes about 2¾ cups.

EACH TABLESPOON: ABOUT 75 CALORIES | 0G PROTEIN | 12G CARBOHYDRATE | 3G TOTAL FAT (2G SATURATED) | 0G FIBER | 6MG CHOLESTEROL | 20MG SODIUM

INDEX

Note: **Bold** page numbers indicate recipes using packaged mixes.

PHOTOGRAPHY CREDITS

Sang An: 135

James Baigrie: 57, 62, 148

Mary Ellen Bartley: 114

Angelo Caggiano: 137, 139

Squire Fox: 7

Brian Hagiwara: 9 (both photos), 11, 104, 145

iStockphoto: 81;
    Jan Bertrem: 12;
    Bill Noll: 13;
    James Harrop: 20, 147;
    Stefanie Timmermann: 37;
    Klaudia Steiner: 39;
    Sorin Alexandru: 61;
    Jill Chen: 64;
    Cathy Britcliffe: 68, 120;
    Tim McAfee: 82;
    Serhiy Zavalnyuk: 97;
    Suzannah Skelton: 131

Rita Maas: 40, 51, 71, 124, 127, 141

Kate Mathis: 16, 92

Steven Mark Needham: 2, 6, 29, 34, 78, 91, 98, 102, 109, 150, 152, 160

Ann Stratton: 94

Mark Thomas: 14 (both photos), 15, 19, 45, 110, 119

FRONT COVER: Rita Maas
BACK COVER: Ann Stratton

METRIC EQUIVALENT CHARTS

The recipes that appear in this cookbook use the standard United States method for measuring liquid and dry or solid ingredients (teaspoons, tablespoons, and cups). The information on this chart is provided to help cooks outside the U.S. successfully use these recipes. All equivalents are approximate.

METRIC EQUIVALENTS FOR DIFFERENT TYPES OF INGREDIENTS

A standard cup measure of a dry or solid ingredient will vary in weight depending on the type of ingredient. A standard cup of liquid is the same volume for any type of liquid. Use the following chart when converting standard cup measures to grams (weight) or milliliters (volume).

Standard Cup	Fine Powder (e.g. flour)	Grain (e.g. rice)	Granular (e.g. sugar)	Liquid Solids (e.g. butter)	Liquid (e.g. milk)
1	140 g	150 g	190 g	200 g	240 ml
¾	105 g	113 g	143 g	150 g	180 ml
⅔	93 g	100 g	125 g	133 g	160 ml
½	70 g	75 g	95 g	100 g	120 ml
⅓	47 g	50 g	63 g	67 g	80 ml
¼	35 g	38 g	48 g	50 g	60 ml
⅛	18 g	19 g	24 g	25 g	30 ml

USEFUL EQUIVALENTS FOR LIQUID INGREDIENTS BY VOLUME

¼ tsp=						1 ml
½ tsp=						2 ml
1 tsp =						5 ml
3 tsp =	1 tbls =		½ fl oz	=	15 ml
	2 tbls =	⅛ cup =	1 fl oz	=	30 ml
	4 tbls =	¼ cup =	2 fl oz	=	60 ml
	5⅓ tbls =	⅓ cup =	3 fl oz	=	80 ml
	8 tbls =	½ cup =	4 fl oz	=	120 ml
	10⅔ tbls =	⅔ cup =	5 fl oz	=	160 ml
	12 tbls =	¾ cup =	6 fl oz	=	180 ml
	16 tbls =	1 cup =	8 fl oz	=	240 ml
	1 pt =	2 cups =	16 fl oz	=	480 ml
	1 qt =	4 cups =	32 fl oz	=	960 ml
			33 fl oz	=	1000 ml = 1 L

USEFUL EQUIVALENTS FOR COOKING/OVEN TEMPERATURES

	Fahrenheit	Celsius	Gas Mark
Freeze Water	32° F	0° C	
Room Temperature	68° F	20° C	
Boil Water	212° F	100° C	
Bake	325° F	160° C	3
	350° F	180° C	4
	375° F	190° C	5
	400° F	200° C	6
	425° F	220° C	7
	450° F	230° C	8
Broil			Grill

USEFUL EQUIVALENTS FOR DRY INGREDIENTS BY WEIGHT

(To convert ounces to grams, multiply the number of ounces by 30.)

1 oz	=	⅟₁₆ lb	=	30g
2 oz	=	¼ lb	=	120g
4 oz	=	½ lb	=	240g
8 oz	=	¾ lb	=	360g
16 oz	=	1 lb	=	480g

USEFUL EQUIVALENTS LENGTH

(To convert inches to centimeters, multiply the number of inches by 2.5.)

1 in	=			2.5cm
6 in	= ½ ft	=		15cm
12 in	= 1 ft	=		30cm
36 in	= 3 ft	= 1 yd	=	90cm
40 in	=			100cm = 1 m

THE GOOD HOUSEKEEPING TRIPLE-TEST PROMISE

At *Good Housekeeping*, we want to make sure that every recipe we print works in any oven, with any brand of ingredient, no matter what. That's why, in our test kitchens at the **Good Housekeeping Research Institute**, we go all out: We test each recipe at least three times—and, often, several more times after that.

When a recipe is first developed, one member of our team prepares the dish and we judge it on these criteria: It must be **delicious, family-friendly, healthy**, and **easy to make**.

1. The recipe is then tested several more times to fine-tune the flavor and ease of preparation, always by the same team member, using the same equipment.

2. Next, another team member follows the recipe as written, **varying the brands of ingredients** and **kinds of equipment**. Even the types of stoves we use are changed.

3. A third team member repeats the whole process **using yet another set of equipment** and **alternative ingredients**.

By the time the recipes appear on these pages, they are guaranteed to work in any kitchen, including yours. WE PROMISE.